A STORY OF GRACE

Holistic Healing after a Diagnosis of Breast Cancer

Nancy Ann Battilega, LPC, CHTP

This book is dedicated to my devoted husband, John, and our four children, Carrie, Tony, Michael and David, who reached beyond their fears to offer me unconditional love and support as I journeyed down the "road less traveled."

NOTES OF APPRECIATION

I'm very grateful to all who read the draft of this book for their thoughtful comments. My husband offered both technical and literary assistance. My daughter suggested I write more honestly from the heart. Friends offered both creative and editorial comments.

My mentor, Ruth Muhr, pointed out parallels to Harry Potter, just as I finished reading the final novel, *Harry Potter and the Deathly Hollows*. I knew that would be the model I would use. I'm also grateful to Barbara Dahl who, in a keynote address at the 2003 Healing Touch convention, compared energy workers to Harry Potter in confronting the "Muggle" world of traditional western medicine with the "magic" of Healing Touch.

I am especially indebted to my supervising psychologist and analyst, Jean Clift, who introduced me to the psychology of the hero journey and encouraged me to write.

Special thanks also to Joyce Rupp, Cyndi Dale and Cynthia Bourgeault for their encouraging words and positive critiques of my initial draft. Authors in their respective fields, their suggestions have helped me produce a more accurate and readable book.

PREFACE

On May 1, 2006, I received a diagnosis of breast cancer. The surgeon, to whom I was referred, recommended an immediate mastectomy. Due to my work in energy psychology I have a strong belief in the body's ability to heal itself. I followed a complementary course of healing for the next sixteen months and tested cancer-free on September 1, 2007.

The surgeon was dismayed at my choice. However, I have practiced nearly twenty years as a licensed professional counselor, with a specialty in trauma. I am also certified in mind/body energy psychology as well as Healing Touch, a form of energy work certified by Healing Touch International. I know of the body's ability to heal itself and of the importance of healing on all levels of being: physical, emotional, mental and spiritual. I felt strongly that I needed to practice what I preach.

Many stories of alternative healing tend to focus on one element such as diet or prayer. I believe that I was successful because I integrated healing on all levels into a well-rounded life. I continued to stay connected to immediate and extended family, friends, neighbors, parishioners, professional colleagues and the broader community. Despite my daily focus on health and healing, this is also the story of a life well lived. It worked!

I have presented many workshops over the years on the Hero/Heroine's journey and know that my story comprises common threads with these mythical giants, both real and fictional. In writing this story I stand on the shoulders of acclaimed writers such as Joseph Campbell, Frank Baum, George Lucas, C.S. Lewis and, more recently, J.K. Rowling. I often related to the character of Harry Potter as I confronted the "Muggle world" of traditional western medicine with the "magic" of Healing Touch.

This is the story of my journey to health and wholeness and the events in my life that prepared me to choose this particular path of healing. I know that each individual is unique and each illness is unique to that individual. There is no "one size fits all" when it comes to cancer or any other illness. Nevertheless, I write in the hope that others, who find themselves in circumstances similar to mine, will be inspired to move through their journeys free from fear, taking all the time necessary to discover what their bodies need in order to heal.

Some of the events in this book may stretch the reader's imagination, but I assure you every word is as true as I can tell it. We each have a unique voice. I have attempted to tell a story which conveys the truth of my journey in a way that others might say, "She is telling my story."

TABLE OF CONTENTS

The Owl Calls My Name

I have always thought May 1ˢᵗ to be an especially beautiful day. Throughout my years in Catholic school we celebrated with flower baskets, May pole dances and sentimental songs to the Blessed Mother. Wherever we've lived I have planted hundreds of bulbs that are usually in bloom at this time. It's also the month my husband, John, and I celebrate our wedding anniversary, my birthday and Mother's Day. May 1ˢᵗ of 2006 will forever more be etched in my mind, not only as the day I was diagnosed with cancer, but as the first day of a miraculous six weeks in which each day brought me a growing awareness of how God is working in my life.

It so happens that on this particular day my good friend, Katherine, has suggested we go to the Denver Botanic Gardens to celebrate my sixty-fourth birthday a week early. Over lunch I tell her how one of my energy partners has seen the archangel Michael standing behind me with his blue sword, strengthening my spine, as though to give me courage. I am puzzled and wonder if that refers to his presence during past struggles. Katherine surprises me further by

1

presenting me with a birthday present (we usually only exchange cards) that she feels "compelled" to give me: a medal of the archangel Michael holding his sword. We are at the gardens when I received the news of the cancer.

I guess no woman ever expects to be one of the unlucky 20%. I certainly didn't. I assure the nurse, who called, that I am okay and promptly start to cry. Thank goodness Katherine is in the car with me. She assures me that I will have all the love, support and prayer that I can possibly use. I am grateful for her comforting words, but it is a while before I am able to drive home.

That night I share the diagnosis with my husband, children and sisters, who are all supportive yet very concerned when I tell them I am choosing complementary health treatments. Friends, relatives and health professionals inundate me with names of local specialists, information on diet, traditional and holistic treatments for breast cancer and a towering stack of books. I am about to venture forth on the steepest learning curve of my sixty-four years. Within a week I am adding minerals to distilled water to increase the alkalinity of my body, altering my diet to eliminate sugar, pesticides and hormones, exercising more faithfully and meditating daily. I lose track of the number of prayer chains to which friends have added my name.

On May 2nd, my husband, John, and I celebrate our forty-second wedding anniversary. He promises to be with me every step of the way and to support my decisions, though it is obvious he personally would have chosen the traditional medical model for himself and would have been relieved had I done the same. Our three eldest children, who live in California, offer to fly home to be with me. They all have some difficulty understanding that, when I say I intend to pursue holistic healing, I am ruling out surgery, at least for the time being.

Fortunately, I have just begun a third level class in contemplative prayer at a nearby retreat center, where I receive much support for this decision. This practice of inviting God to heal past wounds turns out to be a vital tool for me on my journey to health and wholeness.

A friend calls to check on me. She says she had a vision of me, slogging through mud in big rubber boots, and wondered if I have a belief that I have to somehow share the painful experiences of my clients to be an effective healer. I mention this story to my mentor, Ruth Muhr, who shares a "mud" story from one of her former clients. This woman, who had cancer and a propensity for putting others first (like so many of us), envisioned herself as the goddess Kali in the form of a many-titted wolf. Others came to bathe her in healing mud. As she was nurtured by the angels and a multitude of healers, the extra tits fell off. She was healed as she allowed herself to be cared for.

I recall the time John and I took mud baths at the Calistoga Springs. His side of the tub went haywire, and he was covered with bubbles up to and including the pink wash cloth that covered his eyes. It was happy memories like this that helped move me forward on my own journey of healing. I, too, begin to imagine soaking in mud baths at a natural spa, being tended and restored to health by Mother Nature, my angels and loved ones.

I also benefit from a three day anatomy class for Healing Touch practitioners taught by Sue Hovland, who is both nurse and massage therapist as well as a certified Healing Touch practitioner and teacher/trainer. My classmates' healing hands sooth my traumatized, biopsied breast and give me needed courage and energy for the road ahead.

On May 5th I have two dreams. In the first, I see a mother bear and her cub in our condo. The cub is clinging over my right breast. I ask John to pull it off. He says he can't, but I insist. Finally he gets the cub to release its grasp and puts it outside. The mother leaves with her cub. I interpret this to mean that I alone can remove this cancer, and I need to call upon all my masculine strength and determination to be successful.

In the second dream, my son-in-law, Bill, is looking for spray-and- wash to treat a dark red stain on our old, well-worn table cloth. I tell him where it is, but he can't find it. After much searching, I find it right on the table and go ahead and spray the stains, which begin to dissolve. In real life, Bill is a skilled orthopedic surgeon. I believe my intuition is telling me that I can heal this cancer without surgery, but it will take time and effort, and I'll find the solution right there in my own, well-worn, much-used, much- loved body.

That weekend John and I enjoy a night out with a dinner/dance club we recently joined. The following day our youngest son, David, and his girlfriend, Katie, cook a very healthy salmon dinner for us with lots of veggies, salad and no dessert.

On Tuesday, May 9th, my children shower me with fabulous birthday gifts, which shore me up for what I know will be a difficult visit to the doctor's office. The next day the surgeon goes over the results of my MRI, explains my diagnosis of Ductal Carcinoma in Situ (DCIS) and tells me that the dimension of the mass (6x4x2cm) is too large for a lumpectomy. She suggests a mastectomy followed by radiation and tomoxifen. I am reluctant to cut, burn or poison my body and describe my holistic plan of attack. My decision makes her very uncomfortable. However she agrees to follow my care if I sign a release and agree to return in six weeks for an examination and follow-up tests.

This may seem like a hasty or impulsive decision to some. For me it was a choice compatible with my personality, life experiences and professional training. Similar to Harry Potter and countless others who have journeyed into unknown territory, I heard the owl call my name and knew my life would never be the same. I felt compelled to explore options other than surgery. I begin this story by describing the factors which supported my decision to choose complementary methods of healing while working within the traditional medical framework of testing and examination. As with all journeys, the framework for mine lies in the past.

PART I
THE QUEST BEGINS

The Journey

One day you finally knew
what you had to do, and began,
though the voices around you
kept shouting
their bad advice---
though the whole house
began to tremble
and you felt the old tug
at your ankles.
"Mend my life!"
each voice cried.
But you didn't stop.
You knew what you had to do,
though the wind pried
with its stiff fingers
at the very foundations,
though their melancholy
was terrible.
It was already late
enough, and a wild night,
and the road full of fallen
branches and stones.
But little by little,
as you left their voices behind,
the stars began to burn
through the sheets of clouds,
and there was a new voice
which you slowly
recognized as your own,
as you strode deeper and deeper
into the world,
determined to do
the only thing you could do---
determined to save
the only life that you could save.

-Mary Oliver-

1   ✡   *The Empty Nest*

Diagnosis of cancer caused me to reflect back over my life and realize how many unexpected twists and turns there have been. Actually, very little has gone as I planned.

Two years before I received a diagnosis of breast cancer our fourth and last child, David, left home. It was September of 2004. In one month, he was offered his dream job, bought a house and met that "special girl."

John, my husband of forty years, was embarking on an exciting new phase of his career. I was in the process of completing the demanding requirements for certification as a Healing Touch practitioner. We had recently finished the remodeling necessary for me to open a small counseling/ Healing Touch practice from our home. It was with some trepidation, but also a sense of excitement, that I recently left the local Samaritan Counseling Center where I had worked for fifteen years.

I watched David confidently sort twenty-three years of "stuff" into four piles: new home, give away, trash and store in old bedroom closet. My heart overflowed with love and pride for this young man. I hoped that he would, indeed, achieve his dreams, which included eventual ownership of his own small investment company. However, I couldn't help but recall how much my own plans had veered from early dreams.

John and I, high school sweethearts, had dated throughout college and married after I graduated. He was working toward his PhD in mathematics at Oregon State University. I planned to teach until he received his degree, and then we would buy a house in the Portland area and raise the large family we dreamt of, surrounded by friends and relatives. However, before finishing his degree, he got called up for Vietnam. We soon found ourselves, with our fifteen month old daughter, Carrie, on the way to Ft. Benning, Georgia.

After David moved into his own house, I sat in our large, southeast Denver home wondering at all the twists and turns of fate that have brought me to a place so different from what I once imagined. Our three older children and four grandchildren are living in California. We use all the frequent flier miles John accrues on his numerous business trips, but this role of long-distance grandma isn't the one I had once envisioned for myself.

As I pondered my life thus far and wondered what the future had in store for me, I was overcome with a strong desire to travel to Peru. I was somewhat puzzled. John and I have always traveled together. We've spent time in Egypt and Russia and enjoyed several trips to Europe. We've made tentative plans to travel to Greece and Turkey as well as Australia and New Zealand, and even discussed an African photo shoot and a train trip through South Africa. But never Peru.

When I mentioned this persistent desire to hike Machu Picchu and travel through the jungle, John reminded me that he dreads the jungle so much that he chose an airborne unit in the Army over ranger school, despite his fear of heights. Neither the mountains nor the jungles of Peru hold the least appeal for him. He suggested I ask a friend to join me. In September I announced at book club that I was planning to visit Peru come February and extended the invitation. A former neighbor, Kay, expressed interest, and I began to plan our itinerary.

The Empty Nest

2 ⬡ *Peru: The Power of Energetic Healing*

A key factor in my choosing complementary methods of healing to cure breast cancer was the fact that I had experienced the power of herbal and energetic healing in Peru.

The first tours Kay and I attempted to join were filled, so we registered for a small Smithsonian tour on a lovely renovated fishing boat, The Esmerelda. I saw this as a good omen, the emerald being my birthstone. We arrived at our hotel in Lima in the wee hours of the morning on February 6, 2005. After two hours of sleep, we joined our tour of eighteen for a generous breakfast before embarking upon the two hour flight to Iquitos-the central highland city of 500,000 named after an extinct Indian tribe. At our approach I looked down upon a gorgeous patchwork quilt, a multi-hued velvet green, edged in ribbons of yellow, lavender and white. We later discovered that this was a sampling of over two hundred varieties of potatoes, a plant indigenous to Peru.

We arrived in Iquitos on the feast of San Juan during which the children celebrate by dying their skin purple and throwing water balloons. Huge, decorated tree poles gave notice of a dance or party.

Many houses are on stilts, and buildings sit on cement pillars, necessitated by the fact that the tide rises thirty-five feet over the course of a year. Our charming guide, Juan, transported us to the Esmerelda from which we explored a tributary of the Amazon, sighting several species of local birds including a rare falcon and a five-foot iguana.

The jungle is dense along the banks of this tributary. It is comprised of three noticeable layers: a mat of green undergrowth of ferns, small bushes and flowering plants; a middle layer of trees including rubber and mahogany, which house numerous species of monkeys, sloth, lizards and birds, as well as jaguars, and the top canopy of tall, slender trees where the fortunate fauna retreat during the day to enjoy the sun and dry out after the frequent rainstorms. Our initial venture into the jungle was reminiscent of floating down a sparsely populated Louisiana bayou. About the same distance from the equator, both areas are humid, lushly verdant and teaming with creatures that I'd rather see only from a distance.

Grade schools, many with well-maintained soccer fields, are built in clearings along the river banks. We saw beautiful, healthy, dark-eyed children playing soccer while others were paddling homemade canoes between villages and fishing near the shore. Shy little ones clung to their mothers or big sisters and waved at our cameras. We passed one fairly large village of 5,000 inhabitants which had at least one television antenna. Homes in smaller villages are typically three room structures made of reeds and wood with a common area shelter for community gatherings that also serves as an open air market for sales to tourists.

That evening our guides entertained us, after a delicious dinner, with flute, drums, guitar and reed pipes. The steward who played the pipes is known affectionately as "diablito" because he is a 'devil on the pipes'. Juan offered one of many interesting lectures on

14

the geography of the Amazon basin and the variety of ways that jungle plants, insects and animals are interdependent.

Monday morning we woke at 5:30 a.m. for an early morning boat ride. All made use of binoculars to see the iguana, green and brown sloth and the dozen or more varieties of birds spotted by our eagle-eyed guide. Following another hearty breakfast, we visited a small village of three hundred people. Many of the fifty grade school children, on vacation during the three-month rainy season, gathered in their clean and practical cement block school to sing for us. Barefoot and dressed in colorful shorts, shirts and dresses, they happily posed for photos as we distributed school supplies. I treasure my photo with a little girl who told me we share the same name, Nancy.

Villagers went about their daily work of planting, harvesting, winnowing rice and pressing juice from sugar cane using handmade tools they have used for centuries. Older children cared for the little ones while all able-bodied adults tended crops for the quarterly harvest. Fruit is traded for salt, sugar, clothing, kerosene and matches. Our guide said villagers live simply, but peacefully, with little cause for envy-a hard, but stress-free life. However, we all laughed at seeing a teenage boy wearing very large tennis shoes, swinging in a hammock while listening to a transistor radio. Some activities seem to be innate despite cultural influences.

Tuesday morning we ventured out at 6 a.m. to spot thirty of the 1800 species of birds found in Peru. After a hearty picnic breakfast, we shared our leftovers with some local fishermen. I discovered that the graceful black bird with white wings that had encircled me during morning meditation on the prow of the Esmerelda is called a snake bird due to its large, curving neck. I hope she will be the closest I'll get to a snake on this trip.

The highlight of this excursion was the twenty-or-so pink dolphins we spotted on one of the tributaries. They became land-locked centuries ago when a series of earthquakes cut off access to the Pacific Ocean and the Amazon Basin was formed. Our day was filled with wonders: a capybara bathing by the bank, bands of monkeys playing tag through the trees, nocturnal owl-like birds and even a mother caiman surrounded by babies.

Wednesday morning I struggled out of bed, exhausted from having coughed all night long. This was particularly frustrating because I was in excellent health when I left for this trip, planning to enjoy every moment of the cruise and the hike to Macchu Pichu. My concerns about disturbing Kay were groundless; she said she slept soundly through the night. I was pretty miserable the rest of the day, devouring our entire supply of cough drops.

By evening I had a raging fever, a concern to all our companions. I believed I had a bacterial infection and asked our guide if there were antibiotics on board. Some of my fellow passengers offered to share their prescriptions. However, I declined when I heard that we were scheduled to visit a native shaman at a local village the next morning. Juan said it would be appropriate to ask for healing and offered to translate. I decided to pray for healing, since I always have negative reactions to antibiotics.

The climb to the shaman's hut took every ounce of my energy, and I was bright red with fever when we arrived. He graciously answered all questions and then proceeded to bless each individual. When he laid his hands on my forehead, I felt surrounded by love. A sense of complete peace entered my soul, and my fever vanished. The shaman continued to pray and chant over me for about five minutes. He also told me that I had an intestinal infection and that he would send a runner into the jungle to get leaves from the plant that could cure it. I was puzzled about his

16

diagnosis, since I had not experienced any digestive discomfort on the trip, but thanked him graciously for the healing and the offer.

After swimming and resting at a nearby eco-lodge, I returned with the tour to the Esmerelda. That evening I had a light supper and drank lots of anise tea as suggested by the Shaman, whose name is Guillermo. I realized that I had packed tablets of Cat's Claw, an herb I take for a recurrent candida[1] infection. Upon reading the directions, I discovered that it is grown in this part of the Peruvian jungle. Why am I not surprised?!

I sent word to Guillermo thanking him for curing my fever and also for enlightening me to the fact that I needed to be more diligent about managing this candida by eating more intentionally. I then began taking the herbs that I had fortuitously packed. This was the first sign I'm aware of that I was about to face a major health crisis. I included a small gift and donation to support Guillermo's apprentice. He responded with appreciation and promised to send me a blessing.

My night was filled with dreams, and I woke at 3 a.m. surrounded by the most indescribably beautiful shimmering violet blue light. This is the color of the 6th chakra,[2] the energy center located between the eyebrows, the third eye which governs intuition and clairvoyance. I took this to be the blessing offered by Guillermo and was awe-struck. Since beginning Healing Touch training, I had been working on strengthening this chakra and the gifts of intuition associated with it. I had also been told that it is related to the 2nd chakra which governs reproductive organs, emotions, balance of

---

[1] Candida is a yeast infection normally present on the skin, in the intestinal tract and, sometimes, in the genital region. Its presence is often the result of taking antibiotics, which destroy the bacteria that compete with candida, allowing this fungus to grow unchecked. Candida overgrowth is often a precursor to cancer, diabetes, and other immune system diseases.

[2] A chakra is an energy center seen as a spinning wheel of light. There are seven major chakras along the spine, each one reflecting a color of the rainbow. Each governs specific organs in the body as well emotions and beliefs.

masculine and feminine and also organs of digestion and elimination affected by candida.   Evidently, the two days of fever and a cleansing diet of tea, plus taking the Cat's Claw, healed and balanced these chakras allowing me to receive this blessing. I was excited to get back to my practice and see whether or not my intuitive powers would be heightened when working with clients.

I told Juan how grateful I was for the Shaman's gifts, and that I would like to offer something in return. Knowing how difficult it is for him to find the healing plants in his jungle home, which has come under siege from developers during the past decade, I offered money for him to hire labor and buy plants for the medicinal garden he mentioned that he hoped to develop before his death. Our guide was enthusiastic about the idea and promised to convey my offer and stay in touch after my return to the states. We have stayed in touch and, the last I heard, the shaman's garden warded off an attack of army ants and is flourishing. This was such a different journey than I expected; it was everything I hoped for, but so much more!

After returning to Iquitos, we flew back to Lima and enjoyed a sunset tour of the city. With Beatrice as our guide (shades of Dante's "Paradisio") we marveled at the Franciscan Monastery, which is modeled after The Alhambra in Spain and sits atop three centuries of parishioners' bones. (No wonder they used lots of incense during Mass!)   At my request, Beatrice asked our driver to make a short detour so that I could see the church of St. Rose of Lima built on her birthplace. She is the patron saint of Lima and special to me since hers is the name of the parish in which I grew up and my confirmation name. I have always felt a unique attraction to this nun pictured with her arms filled with roses; perhaps this is why I've always had a rose garden wherever we've lived.

On Sunday we flew to Cusco where we stayed overnight in a beautiful, modern hotel to get acclimated to the 14,000 ft altitude.

Coca tea was available for our use and, though Kay and I had little difficulty since we come from the 'mile-hi-city', we enjoyed the tea, nevertheless. We joined other tourists in purchasing beautiful woven goods after watching a family wash, card, spin and weave alpaca wool. Little girls of five were adept at using the drop spindle and weaving on the backstrap loom. We also spent a fascinating hour at an open market where I bought gifts for my grandchildren and some silver jewelry, reportedly hand-crafted by the vendor's uncle, a local shaman.

On our two-day journey to Macchu Pichu we stopped at the village of Willoc. It is located high in the Andes and populated by Inca descendants whom time has passed by. Although the men and boys were playing soccer in modern clothing, the women and girls still wear the hand-woven woolen skirts and flat, black hats of their ancestors and carry both babies and market goods in the woven shawls tied over their shoulders. The villagers are totally self-sufficient, but they do sell handicrafts to tourists, and the children line up enthusiastically for the bread and rolls we brought since that is not part of their diet. Villagers grow no grain; 250 varieties of potatoes, which are indigenous to Peru, are their staple crop.

We stayed at a lovely local hotel and, once again, my sleep was filled with dreams. Having just heard of two murdered men who were discovered with their faces peeled, I dreamt of intrigue and violence between environmentalists, local tribes and corporate interests who hire gunmen to guard their developments. I was a reluctant investigator, and most relieved to wake and discover this was only a dream. The struggle for control of land in the jungle is indeed a dangerous game as was demonstrated by the murder of a Catholic nun, Sister Dorothy Stang, who worked on behalf of the native people and their environment, shortly after I returned to Denver.

This was supposedly the rainy season, but our day long hike among the ruins of Macchu Pichu was photo perfect, and I was grateful for those extra digital discs my husband encouraged me to pack. We were all amazed by the astronomical genius of the Incas and the flawless stone work they created with hand tools over six centuries ago.

The remainder of our visit to Peru was spent exploring a nature preserve where we used magnifying glasses to discover the marvels of the native orchid population, often named with reference to their resemblance to human anatomy. Our guide instructed us in the use of local plants which cure everything from cancer and kidney stones to diabetes and liver ailments. Such natural remedies, healthy diets and lifestyles that include lots of exercise are positive assets that help offset the effects of poverty among these descendents of the once proud and powerful Inca Indians.

Our final day was spent touring architectural ruins and visiting a silversmith. I purchased an exquisite silver llama that took two weeks of exacting craftsmanship to create. As always when I travel abroad, I was torn between my knowledge that I have just scratched the surface and want to experience more and my need to return to reconnect with the people and places that make up that marvelous place called home.

3 ☆ *Spooky: We Are All One*

My deep belief that all life is interconnected was also an
important piece of the puzzle that led me to explore alternatives to
surgery. I knew that the spirit of the universe and every creature in it
would support my body's attempt to heal itself. I relearned this
lesson from an unexpected source.

Upon returning to Denver, I couldn't help but notice that our
cat, Spooky was not doing well. Prior to leaving for Peru I had taken
her to the vet who diagnosed some age-related kidney problems, not
uncommon in a sixteen year-old cat. Spooky had experienced two
traumatic events in recent years that had contributed to this problem.
Three years ago the men who laid our hardwood floors had sealed
off the room with her food and water. The neighbors caring for her
soon rectified the problem, but she let us know how unhappy she was
when we returned. The next incident was more serious; while we
were gone one week she ran out of water and became quite toxic. In
fact, she lost her voice form crying in distress.

As I watched our pretty gray cat with her little white feet stretched out in the sunshine, I recalled the day she came into our lives.

Cats had always been a part of our lives. My husband and I each had had cats as pets when we were kids. Our older children had raised several cats as pets including a tiny black and white cat that survived seventeen years in our rambunctious household.

However, the fall of 1988 found us "catless." Our recently married daughter had moved to Minnesota, our oldest son was in college in San Diego and our second son was beginning college in Wichita. David, our youngest, was just beginning second grade and finding our house unbelievably quiet. His siblings thought he needed a dog but, knowing we would be traveling a lot with children scattered across the country, I decided another cat would be a more sensible choice. Our youngest, with the wisdom of youth, found the perfect compromise: a cat who behaved like a dog!

David and I headed to the local Dumb Friends' League one late October afternoon in search of the perfect pet. There were at least two dozen adorable kittens from which to choose: pure black, fluffy white, black with white paws, blue-eyed Persians, calico striped, each cuter than the next. So what did he choose? The most unattractive, scrawny, runt-of-the litter, mewling gray kitten was the one he wanted. When he picked her up she cried like a terrified baby and clawed her way up over his shoulder and down his back.

I begged him to reconsider, but there was no going back. I had never seen him so determined. We signed the required papers, paid for vaccinations, boxed her up and listened to her cry all the way home.

It soon became obvious that she was indeed the "purrfect" pet. She slept with her master and followed him everywhere. She would trail after him as he left for school and be waiting for him when the school bus dropped him off at 3.15 each afternoon. She sat by his bed on the rare occasions when he was ill and comforted him when he was sad or worried. Spooky had a very hard time when he went away to college. She slept on his bed, awaiting the treasured weekends or vacations when he would briefly reappear in her life.

Now, however, she was definitely suffering from more than strained vocal chords and renal failure. She had barely any appetite and was having great difficulty walking. Suspecting that she was near death, I made an appointment with an energy practitioner who works and communicates with animals intuitively. We talked for thirty minutes on March 1, 2005.

Through Carol I heard Spooky say, "My job is finished now that my master has moved out. I came into this household to be his companion and to teach him things like responsibility and how to be loving and caring. I still have a few things to teach my mistress, but I am nearly ready to leave this world." Spooky also said that she was comfortable and grateful for the good life she had in this family.

She mentioned only two difficult times; these were both times when we were away on extended vacations. She expressed remorse for peeing on our dining room carpet, but felt she was helping me learn some valuable lessons regarding paying attention, patience and humility.

Spooky told us that she was beginning to move into the spirit world. She requested lots of fresh water but little food. She said she would let us know when her time comes by refusing to eat and becoming very apathetic. For now she was content to receive Healing Touch and be able to lie in the sun because both help the arthritis in her back and legs. She expressed gratitude for a very blessed life, but indicated that her service to our family was nearly finished. She made two requests. First, she wanted the comfort of a green light. Second, she said we should adopt another "runt-of-the-litter" from the Dumb Friends League after we've mourned her passing.

After my conversation with Spooky was interpreted by Carol, I made a hasty trip to the grocery store to purchase a green 'party light' bulb. I placed it in the reading lamp near the pillow where Spooky was spending her nights, and she seemed quite content in the warm green glow.

The remainder of the week was unusually warm and sunny for late February in Denver. As the days hovered near 70 degrees, I spent several hours outside cleaning up garden debris in preparation for springtime planting. Spooky walked gingerly across the patio and nibbled on the new green shoots of grass. Saturday morning she basked in the sun on our kitchen floor and seemed to pose proudly while John took a few portrait shots.

However, that afternoon, she failed to come in when I called her. After a thorough search of our back yard, John and I found her curled up in the far corner under our deck. I feared that she had retreated there to die and refused to leave her vulnerable to the wild critters that roam at night. After much coaxing we were able to get her within reach and carry her inside. She could no longer support herself on her hind legs and refused food and water.

After she had rested for an hour, my husband and I watched in amazement as she used her front legs to pull herself up over the eight inch stair into the dining room and then proceeded to crawl some twenty-five feet to our front door. This was an astounding feat for a severely crippled animal. We decided she must be signaling us to call David, who always uses the front door when he comes to visit, whereas we usually use the garage entrance. Though it was Saturday evening and he and his girlfriend were on their way downtown to meet friends, we were able to reach him on his cell phone.

They were at our house within thirty minutes. Our son spent the next three hours stroking his dying cat and letting his only pet know how much he appreciated her loving companionship. I knew by her labored breathing that Spooky was near death. David left to take Katie home, and we agreed to care for Spooky. She took her last breath less than five minutes after he said his final goodbye.

The next day he and Katie came over with a statue of a gray kitten and two boxes of rose petals. Spooky's lovely spirit is with the angels, but her body was laid to rest under the white lilac in our backyard where it rests at peace until returning to the earth from whence it came.

This past spring, a year after Spooky's passing, the white lilac was laden with blooms-a fitting memorial to a loving companion. Neither David nor I have yet adopted another "runt", but periodically a beautiful coal black cat with the shiniest coat of fur appears on our back patio. She grooms herself and sits in the sun for an hour or two and then vanishes as quickly as she appeared. She does not belong to any of the twelve households on our cul-de-sac and none of our neighbors knows where she lives. I consider her periodic presence a very special gift. To this day, sometimes when John or I come home late from a trip and walk into our kitchen from the garage, it feels like Spooky is there, keeping watch and waiting, as always.

PART II
GROWING UP

Last Night As I Was Sleeping

Last night as I was sleeping,
I dreamt-marvelous error!-
that a spring was breaking
out in my heart.
I said: Along which secret aqueduct,
Oh water, are you coming to me,
water of a new life
that I have never drunk?

Last night as I was sleeping,
I dreamt-marvelous error!-
that I had a beehive
here inside my heart,
And the golden bees
were making white combs
and sweet honey
from my old failures.

Last night as I was sleeping,
I dreamt-marvelous error!-
that a fiery sun was giving
light inside my heart.
It was fiery because I felt
warmth as from a hearth,
and sun because it gave light
and brought tears to my eyes.

Last night as I slept,
I dreamt-marvelous error!-
that it was God I had
here inside my heart.

-Antonio Machado (translated by Robert Bly)-

4 ◇ *Awakening to the Goddess Within*

Song of Myself

I believe in you my soul...
the other I am must not
abase itself to you,
And you must not be abased to the other...
And I know that the spirit of God is the eldest
brother of my own,
And that all the men ever born are also my
brothers...and the women my sisters
and lovers,
And that a keelson of the creation is love.

-Walt Whitman (excerpted from 1855 edition)-

Early photos show me to be a beautiful, happy, playful child. However the early years of my life were filled with challenges for my parents. The ways they struggled to cope with physical illness and financial difficulties left a clear imprint on my personality and a confused notion of masculine and feminine traits. On the outside, I was ever the good little girl. On the inside I lost touch with my innate beauty, which left me filled with anger. I was a slowly simmering volcano.

My parents, Evelyn Christman and Edward Scott, were married on January 6, 1939. Times were tough during these pre-war years. When I was three my parents moved with me and my two year old sister, Terri, from Portland, Oregon to the little town of Seaside. Dad began work as a real estate agent and managed the local arcade. When the birth of our twin sisters in 1946 was followed by mother's life-threatening bout with lung cancer, life became very difficult for my parents. Dad was forty-seven, working long hours to support his growing family and struggling with asthma and the chronic sinus infections that would eventually force us to leave this damp coastal town.

However, my memories of these five years are happy ones. Neighbor ladies taught us to bake, iron and play cards and helped mother as much as possible. We lived two blocks from the beach, an endless source of entertainment and exploration. There were parties and parades, clam digging and fishing, and my seventh birthday was held at the penny arcade. I felt I was one of the luckiest girls in the first grade!

Of course my parents' struggles had their effect on us girls, as well, though I was unaware of this until decades later. Mom's near death experience and dad's debilitating asthma attacks left me so fearful that, as a young girl I shut off my feelings lest I be overwhelmed. I made up my mind to work as hard as I could and learn as much as I could to be okay. This was not a bad way to grow up. I was a very energetic young girl who took piano lessons, attempted dance, took part in years of scouting and 4-H activities and excelled in all my studies. I was indeed a really, really good girl. However, I did not become a very sensitive person.

This suited me just fine when I was younger. Leaving home for visits with relatives or camping trips was a great adventure, never marred by feelings of homesickness. Girl Scout camp was a thrill, and I could not fathom the girls who missed their mommies. I was so glad I was not "one of those crybabies." I had my share of teenage embarrassing moments, dating disasters and failures to get some coveted position in high school. The nuns had a lot of power in my small, all girls' Catholic high school. One, in particular, took a dislike to me and refused to give me permission to participate in many school functions. This was incredibly painful for me, but I didn't let myself acknowledge the sadness I felt. Like many young people, I tended to blame myself for not being good enough rather than wonder about what might be going on with this woman that made her so harsh. I just shut all those unpleasant feelings down tighter and tried harder to find the open doors.

Branching Out

Graduation was my favorite day of high school. It was a true Kodak moment as we all walked up to receive our diplomas in long white dresses balancing hoop skirts or yards of crinoline while cradling a dozen red roses in our arms. Many of my classmates were hugging and crying.

Not I. Having just turned eighteen, I was looking forward to my first real job. I would be selling tickets at the train station for a Portland tour company. For the past eight years I had worked each summer picking berries and beans to earn money for clothes and tuition. This summer was going to be so different. Indeed it was. The steady income of a minimum wage was a vital supplement to my full tuition scholarship to Gonzaga University in Spokane and the work/study program in the university cafeteria.

The trade off was enduring four summers of inappropriate behavior from my boss. One memorable incident occurred in the lobby of our new Sheraton Hotel. My 6'2" boss who weighed about 300 pounds, dragged my 5'2´frame across the lobby toward the elevators saying that he wanted to show me the beautifully decorated rooms. I dug in my heels and shouted for help as the entire hotel staff looked on, seemingly paralyzed. I finally broke free with a well-aimed karate chop. Terrified, I ran back to my small office cubicle and secured the door as best I could. The words "sexual harassment" were not yet in the common vernacular. He kept his distance the rest of the summer, and the following year I found a different job with a much nicer boss.

There was a different battle to be fought at Gonzaga University where some of the Jesuit teachers were still having difficulty acknowledging that the college had admitted women. I had to get an A on a mid-term in biology before my professor would deign to answer my questions in class.

Nevertheless, those were wonder-filled years that passed too quickly. John and I had begun dating in high school and continued to date throughout college. We also established close friendships with classmates that continue to this day. Since we were both on financial aid scholarships, we had little money and had to keep our grades up, so many of our date nights were spent at the new Crosby library, named after Bing Crosby, our most famous and generous alum. We also went to every dance and joined friends for beer and pizza and rowdy games of "Spoons" and "Hearts."

I completed my required class work after three years in the Honors Program which waived lower level classes in favor of

Socratic-method study sessions. When John went to Oregon State University to begin work on his PhD in math, I returned to Spokane to complete my secondary teaching certification. In November John, active in ROTC, flew up for the military ball. That weekend President Kennedy was assassinated.

The dance was cancelled, and I remember sitting in a friend's home watching the television replay footage of our handsome, young president being shot and his elegant wife, Jackie, reaching for him in her blood-stained pink Chanel suit. Our world had changed forever. Within five years we would also lose Martin Luther King, Jr. and Robert Kennedy to assassins.

I'm aware that many Americans had lived lives marred with discrimination and violence. My own life had been fairly safe and sheltered, but now our country seemed to have gone berserk. With the death of our beloved Pope John XXIII, Catholics suffered yet another loss, and it sometimes seemed as if the whole world were weeping. I was devastated and felt great sadness and powerlessness. As I looked ahead to our wedding planned for May, I also wondered about the morality of bringing children into such a violent, unpredictable world.

Blooming

Yet individual lives went on. After Christmas I worked as a substitute teacher until our wedding date. We had a large, formal military wedding. John had received a type of commission which required a three year commitment to the military. Many friends drove to Portland from Spokane (some hitchhiked), and we had a grand celebration.

I had planned to teach until John received his PhD, but the birth of our daughter, Catherine Mary, followed by orders to Vietnam, caused us to alter our plan. The next years comprised a difficult series of absences and financial strain. In hindsight, I would have made different choices. These frequent moves were unsettling for all of us, and took a real toll on Carrie's health. However, we did get to see much of our country and learned how "other folks" live.

Like most of our friends, we believed "the action" in Vietnam would not affect us. John had one year left to go at Oregon State University on his PhD thesis in mathematics, and we expected a student deferment. Even when he was called to active duty with the Signal Corps, we hoped for a stateside assignment. However, as the war expanded, Signal Corps officers became in great demand.

Georgia, our first assignment, was an eye-opening and heart-rending experience for both John and myself. Words failed us when we tried to explain to friends and family our horror at seeing the segregated restrooms, drinking fountains, bus stops and restaurants and the abject poverty of so many people, especially blacks. I was very uncomfortable living in the South in the mid-sixties.

Compounding our distress over this social situation was our personal concern for our fifteen month old daughter. Due to the humidity and rapidly fluctuating temperatures, Carrie came down with pneumonia in both lungs. I've never been so frightened as the night I spent bathing her fiery little body in the sink with an alcohol rub, trying to break the fever which had registered as high as our thermometer would go: 106 degrees. Nor have I ever prayed so hard. I'm sure I offered God everything I had or would ever have if He would only spare our baby girl.

John was away on field maneuvers, so I practically lived in Carrie's room at the army barracks which served as the Fort Gordon base hospital. She was eventually discharged, free of pneumonia, but on antibiotics for a strep infection, which I caught. I was again pregnant, having recovered from a miscarriage in April, and was afraid to take antibiotics for fear of harming the baby. In my ignorance, I didn't realize that the estrogen a pregnant mom produces when ill or stressed affects the fetus' developing brain in far more significant ways than would a shot of penicillin.

We left Georgia in December of '66 and drove to Fort Sill, OK, where we managed to rent a two bedroom house on Christmas Eve. Christmas dinner was a stewing hen purchased from the local 7-11, the only store open on that holiday weekend. In April, John was sent to jump school prior to being assigned to the 101st Airborne, The Screaming Eagles. Carrie and I flew to stay with my parents in Portland and await the birth of our son. Tony, christened Edward Anthony after his grandfathers, was born April 21, 1967. A calm, cuddly, happy baby, he seldom cried and slept well. The extra dose of estrogen during the early months of pregnancy may have influenced his disposition; it definitely influenced the fact that he is left-handed and developed an early capacity for connecting to others on a feeling level.

As soon as possible John found an apartment for the four of us in Laurel, MD near his assignment at Ft. Meade. We joined him in May and spent every moment we could together that summer, storing up memories to help us survive the coming year.

After John received orders for Vietnam, I moved back to Portland with Carrie and Tony. We got a small apartment several miles from our parents. Family members and friends visited occasionally, but they were all dealing with major adjustments in their own lives at this time. I felt very much alone and, sometimes, scared. Since I had good health and a teaching certificate, as well as friends and family in town, I knew we would be okay if John did not return. However, I missed him very much and did not want to work full time away from my children if I could avoid it.

Luckily, John returned home physically fit. Whatever emotional wounds he had suffered were kept tightly wrapped, usually surfacing only during occasional nightmares. In the summer of 1970 our second son, Michael, was born, and I began to get more vocal about wanting out of the Army before Carrie began kindergarten. John was frustrated by the amount of red tape that hamstrung his projects so, in 1971 he resigned his commission, and we packed up for the thirteenth time in our six year marriage. We moved to colorful Colorado with five-year-old Carrie and her two little brothers where a good job with an aero-space company awaited John. I settled down to being a housewife, mother, part time student and full time volunteer.

While John was in Vietnam I had begun work on a Master's Degree in counseling, but the behavioral approach then in vogue had little appeal for me. After our youngest started first grade I began working part time at the local junior high school, joined the lecture circuit for various environmental and peace and justice causes and became active in a Catholic lay ministry training organization (LAOS). The year I was appointed director of LAOS I discovered I was pregnant again. Nearly forty, John I were both pleased and anxious.

The next four years are a sleepless blur and were particularly difficult for our sixteen year-old daughter who needed more attention than an exhausted mom had to give. My modus operandi of working hard and intellectualizing my pain was beginning to show huge cracks. I was like Dorothy in the Wizard of OZ, trying to navigate the yellow brick road with a tin man who wasn't even aware "she" was missing her heart. There were also good times. David, nicknamed "Zeke" by his older brothers, became a mischievous delight. Early "Zeke" stories remain a never-ending source of amusement at frequent family gatherings. Carrie left for college, followed two years later by our oldest son, Tony. With our son Michael in high school and David in preschool three mornings a week, I went back to school with a renewed desire to get my Master's in Counseling and Psychometrics.

However, when I scored a "zero" on the anxiety scale of the MMPI (Minnesota Multi-phasic Personality Inventory), my professor suggested I do some self exploration. My own history, combined with observations of my current family, led me to focus on childhood development, family systems and, eventually, Jungian psychology. I interned as a child and family therapist at our local county mental health center and was hired as part of an outreach team upon graduation.

Two years later, after moving across town, I joined the Samaritan Counseling Center, which required six months of individual counseling for each clinician. I began dream work with the respected pastoral counselor and author, Jean Clift. This is when I really started to reclaim my lost self. I had begun dissociating from my emotional center when I was but four years old, building layer upon layer of protective bricks around my heart to safeguard it from the fears, shoulds and oughts that I believed to be true.

I chose to explore my dreams from a Jungian perspective because I was becoming aware of what a distorted view I had of the concepts of masculine and feminine. I had recently spent six months working with in-patient adolescents at near-by Ft. Logan mental hospital. My supervisor pointed out that I tended to expect more of the girls while being more lenient with the boys. Upon discovering that I viewed girls as strong and capable and boys as helpless little puppy dogs, she pointed out that the reverse was nearer the truth. Of course, based on my family history of strong, capable women and seemingly weak men, my view made perfect sense to me. Even in death, at age 91, my mother's strength never faltered.

My father had died of pneumonia twelve years prior in 1988 at age 88. My sister, Terri, visited him in the hospital to tell him how much we girls loved him, what a great dad he had been and how we would all be able to make it without further help from him, basically giving him permission to leave his suffering body. He died shortly after she left, on April 1st. Born of Jewish heritage, having converted to Catholicism shortly before his death and also a life-long practical joker, we figured he deliberately chose this particular date: April Fool's Day, Good Friday and Passover, a rare opportunity for this loving skeptic to cover all the bases.

Mom's death was even more remarkable. After winning, as usual, at her weekly bridge game, she fell one weekend and decided that, having lived to see the new century, she was tired. She went to bed on Wednesday and refused all nourishment. Each of my sisters stayed with her one night and said their goodbyes. I arrived in Portland on Saturday, planning to stay through the weekend. I briefly left mom's bedside to call the airlines about my missing luggage. At that moment the apartment shook and her clock jumped off the shelf and crashed at my feet. I ran back to her bedroom, certain she had died. She was still breathing and evidently just hadn't wanted me to leave. She actually died early Sunday morning with her teeth firmly in place as requested. She was a very strong-willed woman, who both lived life to the fullest and died as she wanted.

About this same time, my recently married daughter came to me and, amidst sobs, asked why I loved her brothers more than her. I was speechless. I had been her Brownie and 4-H leader, attended all her athletic events, sewn all her formal gowns, driven down to college to see her remarkable performance as the Mad Woman of

Chaillot and even flown with her to Florence, Italy to meet the family with which she would be living as an exchange student. I hadn't done nearly as much with any one of her brothers. Finally, I gathered my wits enough to ask her why she felt that way. Her response was that she felt I was more critical of her and less forgiving of her imperfections. Moreover, when I told the boys to do something I always showed then how, but I just expected her to somehow know how to do any given task.

I had to admit this was quite often true. I often took care to show the boys how tasks should be done. I guess I just expected Carrie to learn from watching me or, perhaps, by osmosis, since she, too, is the oldest of four. I started to realize that, despite the fact that I love Carrie every bit as much as her brothers, I had a more difficult time conveying it in a way that made her feel loved. My no nonsense approach to life, somewhat lacking in emotional awareness and gentleness, made it difficult for me to connect with my very emotional, sensitive daughter. The "task oriented" way of showing love indicates how my family history was exerting its influence once again. All the mothers on both sides of my family, as far as I know, have shown love by doing things (cooking, cleaning, sewing, teaching...) rather than hugging, cuddling and nurturing. It would be my task to try to change that modus operandi in myself.

I knew that Carl Jung's psychoanalysis dealt with the animus and anima, and that I had a major challenge ahead of me in order to heal the distorted masculine and feminine parts of my soul. Thus began my relationship with psychologist, Jean Clift, who approaches therapy from a Jungian point of view.

5 ✶ *Digging Deep: Finding My Strengths*

The Hidden World of Dreams

I know that blocked emotions damage our cellular structure, thereby contributing to physical and mental illness. So the effort I put into dream analysis would serve a dual purpose years later when I worked to release the emotions that were feeding my cancer.

Prior to working with Jean I had never paid a lot of attention to my dreams. I was amazed to discover that, by setting my intention to wake after a dream and having paper, pen and a flashlight nearby, I was able to record a wealth of messages from my unconscious self. I first visited Jean in January of 1990. Early dreams were filled with messages from my children and husband to lighten up, let go of the desire to have the perfect family and see each of them as they really are. There were repeated dreams in which I was driving old rattletraps, cars with defective steering, brakes or windshield wipers, in which I have no control or can't see where I am going.

There was an ongoing battle between my head and my heart, and I sometimes felt as though my head would explode. It was a frightening time which became more so as dreams of abandonment and rejection began to surface, and I was forced to come to terms with the effect that my parents' illnesses had on my early development.

By 1991 my dreams had taken a shocking turn with violent imagery that symbolized an intense inner conflict. Dying animals featured predominantly in these dreams. Jean wondered with me about attempts to kill off the free, beautiful, strong part of myself.

One of these dreams was of a house which reflected light and had a cat sitting on a windowsill. Now, in my early 50's I had to decide if this slight warmth of reflected light was all that I could tolerate or feel comfortable with. What would I need to do to weave the warmth of caring and compassion into those pale beams of knowledge and allow true wisdom to emerge?

I began to look for ways to allow myself to be more energized by the Divine Light of love which would cast out the fears that kept me perched, untouchable, on the windowsill. Somehow I would have to find a way to make my cat feel safe enough to let down her guard. I wanted her to be able to merge her aloof, independent self, which was so reluctant to connect emotionally, with the playful kitten who is able to cuddle and let herself be petted.

Light and Shadow

To help me on this journey, God sent into my life a wonderful teacher in the person of Joyce Rupp, author and contemplative nun, who was in the process of gathering material for a new book. We were introduced by some mutual friends, and I attended three of her "days of prayer" over the next few years.

It was from Joyce I began to understand that, despite its positive aspects, too much light is harmful. I thought I already had learned this lesson, having inherited that Irish skin prone to freckles, necessitating constant applications of sunscreen. However, I had little clue about how much effort it was going to take me to temper my overdeveloped Yang energy. I needed to learn how to balance it by strengthening the Yin side of my personality, which is comprised of those darker, feminine energies I had effectively repressed for so many years. During these mini retreats, Joyce reminded us that we all grew in darkness. My first nine months were a time of fantastic growth during which I came to be who I am. Ever since then, my life has been a journey of trying to develop that innate potential.

One of these days of prayer was held during Lent, so we compared these essential dark periods of our lives to the womb/tomb time of Holy Saturday. Joyce used the metaphors of the chrysalis and the time the seed must lie fallow before the warmth of sun and rain and the passage of time concur to allow for transformation. It is a time for trusting, for faith, hope and patience. If we dig it up or crack the shell to take a peek, the new life will die aborning. Like the seed and the caterpillar, we each have the strength we need to emerge from the darkness if we will let go and let God do the work. This is a time to be receptive and accept our powerlessness. Not an easy task for those of us who prefer to be in control.

The following year Joyce facilitated a day of prayer in February on Candlemas with lighted candles to illuminate the soul's journey out of darkness. We discussed Abraham's call to risk a journey into the unknown. I reflected on how powerless I felt in my ability to help my daughter and oldest sons who were struggling with marital problems, career choices and depression. My way of coping with anxiety in the past (just deal with it!) was not working now.

I knew I must turn all these concerns over to God Who created our children, Who continues to shower love and grace on them. I am thankful that we gave them names of powerful saints whom, I trust, are storming the gates of heaven on their behalf. A gift of my Catholic heritage is knowing that my children have guardian angels willing to work overtime on their behalf. This made it easier to acknowledge that their struggles were then (and are now) beyond my ability to fix. I am not in control of their destiny.

Ash Wednesday readings from Joel call us to "re-turn to God with all your heart." When God says "come back to me" it means we have been there before. We lose that sense of connection during our earthly journey, but God never quits loving and inviting us home.

One of the ways we return home to God is by reconnecting with the lost parts of our self. In March I drove to the Sacred Heart Retreat House in Sedalia to hear my friend, author, columnist and educator, Dolores Curran, speak on *Uncovering and Treasuring our True Selves*. Dolores described the exploration of our shadow side as entering a mine. One must go properly prepared, clothed in boots and overalls, with a pick ax and headlamp. It's a messy job, but the rewards are great. For those willing to work hard, there are nuggets of gold and silver hidden in the rocky caves.

With the words of my friends encouraging me on, I began to explore other tales of struggle, dark journeys and home comings.

Though my nights were filled with incredible dreams, real life moved me forward from day to day. Carrie had married and finished her law degree at Georgetown Law School. Tony's dreams of being a professional baseball pitcher came crashing down when he broke his leg playing baseball in Sweden the summer he graduated from the University of San Diego. He earned a teaching certificate and got a job teaching and coaching at Rancho Bernardo H.S. in northern San Diego. Michael survived a serious accident during his freshman year away at college and transferred to Mesa State in

Grand Junction, CO. David, then 10, John and I were all excited to be able to see Michael more often and attend his college ballgames.

Strong, Lonely Women

Our counseling staff at Samaritan began working on genograms. I studied mine, filled with strong pioneer women, the eldest in their families, who survived by working hard and outwitting nature. I am descended from a long line of women who think and work hard and have little time or inclination to honor their feelings.

This poem is a tribute I wrote to their strength and courage:

The Silver Gate

I am my great grandmother
who rode the waves from Ireland and
defeated smallpox,
a survivor.

I am my grandmother
who pioneered the Oregon trail,
tilled the soil and tended store,
a survivor.

I am my mother
who endured quarantine and Depression
to rise above, thrive and prosper,
a survivor.

I am birthed through this same silver gate,
touched yet untouched by their shared fate
of hardship and innate courage to create
a richer dowry for my generation.

Over and over I pass through this gate,
devouring the afterbirth of my re-creation.

The dreams kept coming. They began to focus on a stifled need for nurturing, a result of that underdeveloped heart aspect that had been passed down through the generations on the female side of my family tree. This batch of dreams is full of children chasing after parents who drive away, shopping trips where nothing is purchased and visits to restaurants where no one eats. Jean challenges me to stop looking to others to meet these needs and open my own heart. I know I must learn to love and nurture myself, but have little clue how to go about this daunting task. This is definitely one of these times where I will have to "fake it 'til I make it."

I've never had a professional manicure, hate to shop and seldom get my hair done. I relax by playing the piano, reading, sewing and gardening, but I must admit these are all "productive" rather than "playful" hobbies. I wander through "Toys are Us" to see what speaks to me. I am overwhelmed by excess and leave with a jump rope and a bottle of bubbles.

One of the repercussions of having repressed my "feeling" side, and over-developed the more masculine "doing" side of my personality, was that I had spent little time developing friendships with other girls during my school years. Since I had three sisters, I didn't perceive this as a great loss at the time. There were two girls in grade school with whom I shared a May birthday; Kathleen, Joyce and I have remained good friends to this day. However, being a father's daughter, I was a bit of a flirt, and turned most easily to boys for companionship and conversation.

My college years were so filled with long hours of study and work that every free minute was spent with John, and I barely noticed how few women friends, other than my roommate, I made during that time. A brief exception was our two years of grad school at Oregon State in Corvallis. Newly married and pregnant in the fall of '64, I relied heavily on the other young moms in similar situations for support and companionship. We gave showers, exchanged babysitting and baby clothes, played cards, entertained with inexpensive potluck parties. They were the ones who wrapped my bleeding body in blankets and rushed me to the hospital when my second pregnancy ended in miscarriage.

Once we left this environment for military life, forming friendships became a painful ordeal; no sooner did I reach out to a new neighbor, than I found myself packing up to move across the country.

However, as the children grew, and we finally bought a home and settled in Denver, friendships were fostered through church, sports, scouting, PTA and my book club. I didn't really understand what I had missed during my childhood years until, as a counselor, I started hosting mother/daughter workshops. These were always fun sessions and eye-opening for me. I began to see what incredible strength these moms drew from their friends and how important healthy friendships were for the girls in overcoming the pervasive sense of loneliness and isolation in our modern American society.

Out of these presentations grew my desire to build a day of retreat based on the concept of female friendships. I was now in my early 50s and had many good friends, including a group of spiritual friends from my church. We called ourselves the Christianas and met monthly at the home of my friend, Katherine Claytor, also a wife and mother as well as a spiritual director and former nun. Sometimes Katherine joined me for these friendship presentations to share the ways in which she and three special friends have shared one another's joys and sorrows over the past thirty-some years.

Then came the day when I was diagnosed with Bells Palsy. This is a condition in which the facial nerve is paralyzed, causing the eye to droop and the mouth to go slack. Besides looking grotesque, the recipient loses the ability to protect her eye through blinking, can't modulate incoming sound, loses the sense of taste and has difficulty forming certain letters of the alphabet. Katherine and I were scheduled to do a day of prayer on the topic of women's friendships at Sacred Heart Retreat House in six weeks. She went on a pilgrimage for me, and friends stormed the gates of heaven with prayer on my behalf. I prayed I would be among the lucky ones who recover in six weeks. No such luck!

We went ahead and did the workshop. I remember looking up from my notes scattered with such words as female, friendship, freedom from fear, etc. and saying to these women from church, assembled for a day of quiet reflection, prayer and story-telling, "There's no way I can present a workshop on female friendships when I can't wrap my tongue around the f...ing letter "F". That was my last workshop for several years.

PART III
WANDERING IN THE FOREST

The Inferno

Midway in our life's journey, I went astray from the straight road and woke to find myself alone in a dark wood. How shall I say what wood that was! I never saw so drear, so rank, so arduous a wilderness!

Its very memory gives a shape to fear.

Death could scarce be more bitter than that place!

But since it came to good, I will recount all that I found revealed there by God's grace.

-Canto I, The Inferrno, of *The Divine Comedy*

Dante Alighiere, translated by John Ciardi-

7   Bell's Palsy: Exploring Alternative Healing

*"Trouble makes us one with every human being in
the world...Trouble creates a capacity to handle
it...meet it as a friend, for you'll see a lot of it..."*

-Oliver Wendell Holmes as quoted   by Isabel
Leighton, *A Treasury of New Words to Live By* (p.46)-

July 20, 1997. As I review my notes, journal and day-timer
schedule for that year, I am amazed at the pace of my life ten years
ago.   There were days when, on top of a fairly full counseling
schedule, I was often giving presentations or attending classes during
the evening and on weekends.   That spring I had caught a staph
infection that settled in my eyes, not unusual for those in my family
with an inherited dry-eye condition.   I took antibiotics to which I
developed an allergic reaction, but just added antihistamines and
kept going.

There was a trip to California in March to celebrate
birthdays, Easter in Portland, a balloon ride, and a flight to Boston to
watch our oldest son run the marathon.   Then came May with my
birthday, wedding anniversary and Mother's Day celebrations plus

all the gardening, which I love though it can be exhausting. June brought Father's Day and David's sixteenth birthday, hours behind the wheel and a search for a reliable used vehicle. We also accompanied him and his team on many baseball road trips.

During a 4th of July tournament in Steamboat Springs, an incomparable gem in Colorado's treasure chest, John and I were enjoying a lovely trout dinner at a charming little café by the proverbial babbling brook. I recall commenting on how blessed we were to have good health, jobs we loved and four wonderful children. I should have remembered to knock on wood. The next day we took David to the E.R. with a raging fever caused by a virulent strep infection. Leaving his tournament early, over tearful protestations, we arrived home to find that a leaky pipe had caused our kitchen floor to warp and flooded David's basement bedroom.

I spent the following week interviewing contractors and was on my way to secure the loan for remodeling when I started to feel "not myself." I looked in the mirror and nearly died of fright. The left side of my face had gone totally slack, and I had gone from a young-looking 55 to a haggard-looking 70 year-old in a matter of minutes.

A massage therapist/chiropractor friend made the diagnosis of Bell's Palsy, a disease of which I had never heard. She also suggested I go to the ER to rule out a stroke. The ER staff confirmed the diagnosis, prescribed a week's supply of Prednizone and an anti-viral drug, and referred me to the first of three neurologists I would see over the next several months.

Having been in good health my entire life, I was initially hopeful that I would recover quickly. However, as six weeks became six months, little changed, and the neurologists seemed puzzled. I soon learned that there is really nothing western medicine can do to cure this disease. Eastern medicine calls it "the wind disease", and people often contract it after being out in extremely cold weather, having an air conditioner blowing on them or leaning against a cold window. A large majority of cases are caused by the same herpes virus that causes chicken pox and shingles. This was true in my case, and I feel very blessed that I did not have to cope with the pain of shingles as well.

I had never thought of myself as an especially vain person, but this disease challenged my belief that "looks don't matter." I frightened kids at Halloween even without my mask; the woman seated next to me at a wedding dinner moved as far away as possible; new clients failed to return and when, the following March, Girl Scouts and Brownies looked away rather than pursue me to sell cookies, I came home from the store in tears.

My family and friends were consistently supportive. My husband continued to take me out to dinner, movies and plays, even though I complained of loud noises and had to slurp my food. Carrie sent me cards, a bookmark and photos of me smiling (my biggest loss) and a journal in which she encouraged me to write. Did I ever! The words poured forth as I tried to figure out the whys: Why me? Why this? Why now? But most of all I struggled to figure out how: how I could heal, how I could grow from this and how I could make darn sure I never got it again! My son Tony, in researching Bells Palsy on the internet, discovered a man who had contracted it four times. I was appalled and resolved that once was definitely enough for me.

My journey into alternative medicine began. I tried the twelve session routine recommended by acupuncture for "wind diseases" to no effect. Actually it did help balance my energy and relax the right side of my body which had been overcompensating and working too hard. I started getting a massage every two weeks to help my body recover from this trauma and relax my shoulder which had become almost immobile. Acupressure treatments brought some relief, so I took a class to learn to work on this facial nerve myself. A gifted naturopath and intuitive healer near my home gave me both hope and good advice on self care and supplements to strengthen and detoxify my body.

All of these talented professionals offered gifts which contributed to my healing, and some I continue to see. But the real breakthrough in this journey was a massage I received on a women's retreat by a Healing Touch practitioner, Nancy Burns. Nancy is a nurse, massage therapist and Healing Touch trainer who strongly encouraged me to take the necessary training to become a certified Healing Touch practitioner. I had real doubts that I had any such gift, but she was insistent that it would facilitate my own healing and be a positive complement to my psychotherapy practice. She was right on both counts.

I took my first level of training shortly after meeting Nancy in the fall of 2003, and was surprised beyond words to discover that I could "see" energy. Even more important to me personally was the growing awareness that there is an energetic component to all illness. Healing Touch views all illness (physical, mental or emotional) as resulting from stuck energy.

As a psychotherapist in a holistic practice, I have always been aware of the interconnectedness of mental, physical and emotional health. Somehow, in my own case, I had only focused on what was going on with me physically prior to my illness. I had noted the busy life, the infection and various stressors that had depleted my immune system, allowing this opportunistic disease to invade my body. I really hadn't paid much attention to what had been happening with me mentally, emotionally and spiritually prior to that time. Now I began to wake up.

About this time Louise Hay came out with a new edition of her classic *Heal Yourself*. Unlike her previous edition which I reference often, the new one listed Bells Palsy: origin-unexpressed anger.

I thought I had explored this topic thoroughly during those many counseling and supervisory hours with Jean. However, determined that one go-round with this disease was going to be enough for me, I set an appointment to make sure there were no angry stones left unturned.

Dreams continued

Jean, who herself had suffered an attack of Bells Palsy many years ago, and I both agreed that this disease has a component of unacknowledged anger. I have learned that anger and sexual energy are usually dealt with in similar fashions in our culture; these feelings often make us uncomfortable, and we tend to either repress them or push them onto others in an explosion of destructive energy.

My dreams reflected this connection. Some were filled with anger, but others were blatantly sexual. The latter were typically Freudian, filled with smokers, diners, cigars and food. Others, which I found really disturbing, dealt with bi-sexual and homosexual issues. I was repeatedly confronted with sexual advances from women I viewed as strong, capable and successful. I worked to change my view of my sexuality to that of a pleasurable gift and of sexual intercourse as an opportunity to both give and receive, to nurture and be nurtured in return. This is a new concept for me and is probably a somewhat foreign idea for many women of my generation who had the words "Good girls don't" engraved upon their minds and souls, if not their foreheads.

There were also numerous dreams about children being frustrated at play or needing to be rescued. Sometimes I would be rescuing babies or children stranded by floods. In a number of dreams, it would be our youngest son, at various ages, in danger from people or risky endeavors.

Then one day I had a dream so scary and powerful that I woke up sobbing. I was dressed in the gingham gown and bonnet typical of pioneer days and surrounded by a tall, wooden, stockade fence. My task was to sort wheat from weeds (similar to the first task of Psyche as she tries to win back Cupid). Bunnies and chicks are running around my skirt, when I look up and notice a large gray wolf trying to break in. Two men, who look like my husband and father, say they are sorry that they can't help and leave me to fend for myself. I have only scissors. I stab the wolf twice in the neck, but it can still talk. With a voice that sounds like my son Tony it cried, "Mommy don't keep loving me; put me out of my pain." The wolf was incredibly beautiful. It bled a lot and finally died. By the time I was fully awake, my pillow was soaked in tears.

Jean helped me see that all these dreams were attempts to integrate the masculine and feminine aspects of my soul (anima and animus). This was such a difficult task because I was struggling to change messages that had been passed down through generations on both sides of my family:

- To be feminine is to be remote, strong and lacking in empathy.

- To be masculine is to be loving but weak.

- To be playful is to be at risk, maybe even stupid.

I want to believe differently, both for myself, for the sake of my marriage, and for the health of my children. I really want to model a healthier message for my children and in my relationship with John. I began to work on ways that John and I can play together.

I don't want to raise a daughter who believes that to be smart and successful, she must also be emotionally remote and lonely. (Fortunately, she is both smart and successful and also emotionally aware.) And I do want to raise kind, thoughtful sons, who are also strong and capable. My mind struggles to release the old dichotomies and think differently about the roles of the sexes and how masculinity and femininity can be integrated into a whole, healthy personality.

In *The Heroine's Journey*, Maureen Murdock writes:

> *Your inner man and inner woman*
> *have been at war*
> *they are both wounded*
> *tired*
> *and in need of care*
> *it is time*
> *to put down the sword*
> *that divides them in two.*

I was beginning to get this concept intellectually, but my whole self had not yet grasped it fully, and I continued to have violent dreams. In another memorable animal dream I am sitting in a circular forum, like that in the Italian town of Assisi, by a fountain that has gone dry. A black and white cat approaches me. I try to knock it unconscious, but can't. Then I slit its throat with scissors. There is a lot of blood, but the cat is still alive. Finally, I stab it in the heart. I wake up in a cold sweat, feeling a chasm of sadness, with my heart beating wildly.

This dream is screaming at me that I am killing some part of myself. I explore it from several aspects. I became smart and emotionally distant to survive. That was safer both at home and in the Catholic school system, where to speak up invited punishment and ridicule. So I became silent and kept my feelings held tightly. Our early married years were so chaotic that I felt I couldn't afford to be seen as needy which might again invite rejection or criticism, so I became stoic and, to a certain degree, even heartless and unfeeling toward myself and, unfortunately, my infant daughter when John was in Vietnam. Unable to comfort myself, since I was so disconnected from my feelings, I couldn't comfort her.

I also wonder, "What part of me does the cat represent?" Can I approach John, pull in the claws and still stay safe? Can I be that cuddly kitten, or do I always have to be on guard with my back arched and my hair electrified? This cat didn't die willingly or easily. I knock it on the head (shut off feelings and emotions by intellectualizing), but it is still alive. I try to domesticate and silence it by cutting its throat with scissors (give up political activism at John's request and focus on house, kids, Scouting and other volunteer work), but it survives. Finally I stab it in the heart. Can I recover from this fatal wound? How does one mend a torn heart? I have much work to do!

I began by deciding to concentrate on ways that John and I could spend more fun time together. Within the year we were invited to a wedding in California and spent time on the boardwalk at Santa Cruz where we grabbed for the brass rings at the Merry-Go-Round and shared root beer floats at the A&W drive-in as we had when we were first married. Soon the first of our four grandchildren made her arrival, giving us even more reason and opportunity for fun family get-togethers. We took the children on great vacations, but also enjoyed traveling to romantic places like Spain and France on our own.

We took up dancing, joined a formal dinner-dance club and bought cowboy/girl boots so that we could go country-Western dancing on weekends. John enjoys ballgames and fishing with our sons, and I prefer plays and an occasional opera or ballet with my daughter or girlfriends, but we share these delights and once in a while we join one another at a special event. We celebrated our fortieth wedding anniversary three years ago by taking the entire family on a twelve day cruise of the Mediterranean which was such a wonderful, once in a lifetime experience that I don't think we'll ever get tired of talking about it.

As we approached our forty-second anniversary in May of 2006, I was thinking that life could hardly be better. Dancing kept us both fit and in good health; we had a lovely home and jobs that we loved as well as really good relationships with our children who seemed to enjoy spending time with us and one another. What more could anyone want? I had a vague sense of having felt this way the summer I got Bells Palsy.

7   ✡   *Michael: Unlocking My Fears*

"The Soul is Here for Its Own Joy"

-Rumi-

The last Sunday in April our son, Michael, called. For many years Michael was our "anxious" child-the one who carried a symptom the rest of the family could not acknowledge. This time, he was the catalyst for my willingness to confront my own fears.

Michael and I have what, for lack of a better word, might be called an "interesting" dynamic. Our conscious relationship began the day I went into labor in 1970. My water broke mid-afternoon, conveniently just after my husband's sister, Mary, arrived at our Virginia home, having flown in from Oregon to help care for Carrie and Tony. This baby's due date wasn't until the 21st of the month, the same as his brother and sister. However, my mother had told me she was having trouble remembering the birthdays of all her grandchildren. Since my sister had delivered a darling red-headed baby girl two years earlier on July 14th, mother thought it would be convenient if I would have this child on that date also.

Ever the good and dutiful daughter, I tried. I watched the minute hand on the clock on the wall as it moved from 11pm to 11:15 to 11:30 to 11:45. At 11:59 I focused on the second hand as it jerked its way toward midnight and prayed that Michael or Michelle would get a move on it. Evidently sensing his mother's increasing agitation, Michael poked his little red head out just in time for a recorded birth date of July 14, 11:59:59, one second before midnight on Bastille Day. Born under the sign of Cancer, the crab, he was a fighter from the get-go, and I adored him from the moment I laid eyes on him.

Physically, whereas our other children resemble their German/Italian heritage, Michael, with his fair complexion and golden red hair, is a carbon copy of my Scots-Irish father. Temperamentally he differed from his older siblings as well. They were extraverted and gregarious, always up for the next adventure and easy travelers. The minute we turned the ignition in the car, they both fell asleep. Not Michael. He was more shy and quiet and preferred staying close to home. As soon as we put him in the car he started to wail and flail his little arms and legs until he turned red from the top of his head to the tips of his toes. Nothing I could do would console him. I feared he would asphyxiate himself during the drive from our home in Falls Church to my uncle and aunt's home in Long Island for his baptism.

Michael's shyness and lack of comfort in new situations turned out to be the result of deep-seated anxiety that was finally diagnosed in first grade. We tried counseling at the local mental health center, but that was a disaster. Michael refused to go and, since neither John nor I were impressed with this young, unmarried counselor who seemed bent on looking for someone to blame, we didn't force the issue. Skilled family counseling would have been a godsend to us. As it was, Michael struggled through his fears with sheer will-power and as much love and support as we knew how to give.

He is also my opposite in many ways which, at times, has made communication difficult. On the Myers-Briggs his personality type is an introverted, sensate, analytical and spontaneous ISTP, whereas mine is his mirror image, the more extroverted, intuitive, feeling and very goal-orientated ENFJ. Our astrological charts are both lovely, but he is a fiery Cancer, and I am an earth-bound Taurus. Just as he likes and needs friends, fun and freedom, I am more comfortable with home, garden, stability and security. When I try to talk to him I am facing my own shadow and vice versa. However, despite my failure to appreciate his gifts at times, he has grown to become a loving son and a kind and successful young man. I am truly indebted to Michael for carrying the shadowy aspects of my self that I needed to own and embrace-all those fears and anxieties I had stuffed deep inside and refused to look at since four years of age.

So when he called the last Sunday in April of '06, I thanked him for being my angel, for the times he carried the worries and fears I was too weak or oblivious to accept myself. He, of course, told me that I must have the wrong son on the phone! (He also has a good sense of humor.) I repeated that I wanted him to know that I could hold my own and wished to free him from any concerns he might have to the contrary. He said thanks, because he had enough trouble just taking care of himself, and we laughed.

A few days later I discovered that a routine mammogram, done the previous week, was "suspicious", and I would have to have several biopsies. Now I would see if I did, in fact, have the courage to face my own fears. My promise to Michael was soon to be tested.

Michael: Unlocking My Fears

I took it as a good omen that my primary therapist was named Grace. I was somewhat discomforted by the blood from the biopsies that oozed out of my poor right breast when it was squeezed between those plexi-glass sheets during the follow-up mammogram. What are they thinking? However, I never experienced any significant pain, even when the anesthetic wore off. I took it easy all afternoon. Fortunately it rained, and my hiking group cancelled our monthly outing, so I didn't even have to feel bad about missing our hike. John took me out for sushi and then we joined our Friday night dance group to hear one of our better country/western bands play. We danced for a couple of hours, but saved our more aerobic moves for a later date.

The next day I decided to visit two nearby department stores to look for a comfortable skirt or dress in which to dance. All the clothes appeared ugly, garish and shapeless. Normally I see beauty wherever I am, so I returned home thinking a good lunch would perk me up. Nothing looked appealing except the chocolate praline cookies left over from our dinner party earlier in the week. Not a good option! With energy at low ebb, I picked up my copy of Anne Lamont's *Traveling Mercies*, curled up with a cup of tea and began to read her chapter on *The Mole*. By the time I finished, I had a whole new perspective on having to wait through the weekend to get my biopsy report. I had been beating myself up for not being totally positive with my 80% odds. She writes of not being content with 98% odds. My guess is that, until we get that all-clear phone call from the pathologist, 99.99% odds are not reassuring enough. After all, someone has to be in that .01%.

I was so positive that I would be among the lucky 80% that I rehearsed what I would say to Ashley when she called to give me the good news. I was already prepared to let the Sally Jobe Breast

Center know how incensed I was because my poor right breast had been needlessly traumatized due to a false positive. I should have been so lucky!

As the reader now knows, I not only was not in the lucky 80%, but mastectomy was the only viable option offered by traditional medicine. After agreeing to the surgeon's terms for a follow-up exam and tests in June, I joined my husband for a few days in Hawaii where I met with a native healer and began to develop an initial plan of attack which gradually evolved into a long term strategy for health and healing.

Michael: Unlocking My Fears

PART IV
CONFRONTING THE DRAGON

The Road Not Taken

Two roads diverged in a yellow wood,
And sorry I could not travel both
And be one traveler, long I stood
And looked down one as far as I could
To where it bent in the undergrowth;

Then took the other, as just as fair,
And having perhaps the better claim
Because it was grassy and wanted wear;
Though as for that the passing there
Had worn them really about the same,

And both that morning equally lay
In leaves no step had trodden black.
Oh, I kept the first for another day!
Yet knowing how way leads on to way,
I doubted if I should ever come back.

I shall be telling this with a sigh
Somewhere ages and ages hence:
Two roads diverged in a wood, and I-
I took the one less traveled by,
And that has made all the difference.

-Robert Frost-

8   ✡   *Pele's Presence: May 11, 2006*

As Kingfishers Catch Fire

As kingfishers catch fire, dragonflies draw flame;
As tumbled over rim in roundy wells
Stones ring; like each tucked string tells, each hung bell's
Bow swung fins tongue to fling out broad its name;
Each mortal thing does one thing and the same:
Deals out that being indoors each one dwells;
Selves---goes itself; myself it speaks and spells,
Crying What I do is me: for that I came.

-Gerard Manley Hopkins-

This is one of the more unforgettable days of the initial six-week period following my diagnosis. I am planning to meet with three fellow Healing Touch practitioners to meditate and exchange treatments as we have been doing twice a month for the past year. I feel a strong intuition that the crystal, selenite, might help me heal. I know little about crystals, but call my friend, Franny, who lives in

Parker. She is already on her way to our session; lo and behold, she has a huge selenite crystal on the seat beside her! During our work together that morning she sees Christ and the angels ministering to me.

Late that morning, I receive a second treatment from a remarkable energy worker, Gina Fenske, who does angelic healing. Under her guidance I visualize a perfectly healed breast in shades of pink and emerald green, the healing colors of the heart chakra, which influences all health issues in the area of the chest. We also work on my digestive area. I have become aware that Guillermo, the shaman in Peru, was warning me to cure the candida I have suffered from for years because it is a known precursor to cancer. Gina says that my digestive system is also challenged by all the information I am trying to digest so rapidly, as well as by fear.

God has protected me from fear of the cancer. I have been blessed by a real feeling of peace and certitude that all will be well. However, I seem to fear that, if I get well and claim my power as a healer whom God works through, I will lose something. Perhaps people will think I'm crazy? Many folks are not comfortable with the notion of women healers, especially our more traditional churches. I work with Gina to send loving energy to heal the digestive organs and release all fear.

I begin to explore my fears. Can I deal with being thought of as a kook? How will my relationship to my Healing Touch community change? After all, most of my co-workers are nurses and support traditional medical practices. How will this affect my relationship with John, my children and grandchildren? How will my own life and psychotherapy practice change? I am already aware that this experience has radically changed the way I view illness. I also notice that I crave solitude and that, in both my work as a psychotherapist and as a Healing Touch practitioner, I tend to work more from the heart and less from the head. These are big changes for a former extrovert, teacher and public speaker.

Gina comments on the fiery heat trapped in that region of my body. It is so intense that it reminds her of Pele who, she informs me, is the Hawaiian goddess of volcanoes. Having been to Hawaii, I know the story of this beautiful 13th Century warrior princess who was trapped in a cave and died during a volcanic eruption. I resolve to use this fiery energy to purify my body of the candida and cancer but, deep in my heart, I realize that only love will transform my illnesses. I must become a heart-centered warrior and overcome this cancer with love rather than force.

Later that day I meet two friends from our neighborhood book club who have offered to pray over me. Charlene and Pam are powerful prayers. When they ask me what my immediate plans are, I mention that John has invited me to accompany him on a business trip to Hawaii. Charlene replies, "You must go. I know a healer in Hawaii who works with the energy of Pele, the Hawaiian goddess of volcanoes." This healer lives and works on Maui, and the only day we could visit her would be a Saturday, but I take her number just in case.

That evening a former co-worker calls from Grand Junction to wish me a belated happy birthday. Knowing she visits Hawaii whenever possible, I tell her I am thinking of joining John there. She replied, "I just had a dream that I was with Pele, the Hawaiian goddess of volcanoes, at the creation of the world. You must go. The islands have such wonderful healing energy."

Never before have I heard a person in the lower forty-eight states mention this Hawaiian goddess. Most stateside folks think of a soccer player when the name Pele is mentioned. To hear it spoken of three times in one day in this context is, needless to say, quite remarkable.

John agrees to arrange a side trip for us to visit Maui on Saturday the following week if I can get an appointment with Kapua. To my delight she is working that day and has one opening. I sign up.

I join John in Hawaii the following week. He takes some time off, and we enjoy five wonderful, carefree days of R&R. My session with Kapua is lovely, and she suggests that I study techniques of shamanic journeying and avail myself of sound healing to break patterns of communication between the cancer cells.

I take her advice. I find books and a guided meditation to assist in shamanic journeying. I call a Healing Touch practitioner in Boulder who has a specially designed table with chimes and a keyboard to use for sound healing. Visiting her is a very soothing experience. I often use the CD she gave me to go into a trance where deep healing and relaxation occurs.

After returning from Hawaii I continue to feel God's hand guiding me every step of the way. One night I dream that I am lecturing on how I used energy medicine to overcome breast cancer. When I awake I draw the "new career" card from my deck of archangel cards which I use periodically for inspiration. At this point I have no idea what that new career might be (Writer? Speaker? Healer? Teacher?), but the thought brings me comfort, hope and a myriad of possibilities.

That night I meet with my contemplative prayer group and am again reminded about how my healing journey parallels our life journey in that both demand total trust in God to successfully reach one's goal.

On Wednesday I take a break from study and work to putter in my garden and see my chiropractor. He says my body is having a hard time keeping pace with the rapid energy changes and works to balance my spine, organs and nervous system. It feels good to be grounded because I have felt, lately, that I've been rather "bouncy." Bouncy may be great for Tiggers, but it's a rather uncomfortable feeling for those of us born under the sign of Taurus, who prefer to keep our feet on the ground.

Over the next several days I reflect on Gina's message. I assist my digestion in every way possible by watching my diet, taking advantage of massage and Healing Touch techniques and using the ion cleanse machine I bought last year to help detoxify my organs. Confident that I will recover from this cancer, I know that I have the potential, with God's grace, to become a powerful healer. In order to claim that power I must release all fear and let go of the need to control and the need to know with certainty. I must be able to step into the unknown and trust God.

I am having some real trouble with this as my left leg and left foot have been causing me a lot of difficulty. Monthly visits to my massage therapist and chiropractor over the last six months have been focused on trying to balance my hips and find the source of the stabbing pain in my foot. It seems my body knew well before I was aware that I would have to walk this particular path, and it wanted nothing to do with it. As if I had a choice!

During my next treatment with Gina I see myself wrapped in a red blanket as though I am being cleansed and purified by fire. She says she sees a book growing out of the flames, and we discuss my resistance to the dedication and discipline it would take to write and publish. I'm not at all certain I want to embark upon such an endeavor, but I must admit that I am accumulating a wealth of information which it would be nice to share.

On Saturday, May 27th, I meet with Jodi Reed, a graduate of the Barbara Brennan school of energy medicine. I had met with Jodi a year ago as part of my Healing Touch certification program. At that time she said she had once known me by the name of Rose and that, when I work from my heart I emit rose-colored energy. When I work from my head, the former teacher, I emit a yellow-green energy. My job, she said at that time, was to integrate these two aspects of my personality. She suggested that the task before me is to learn to be equally comfortable working from either head or heart as the situation warrants.

What I found interesting about this exchange is that I had just returned from Peru where I went out of my way to visit the church of St. Rose of Lima because that is my confirmation name. Of course, Jodi had no way of knowing that.

So I anticipate that this second visit to Jodi will be very interesting. I am not disappointed. We begin by using the fiery red-hot energy of the volcano to clear out unhealthy cells from the breast, but meet with some resistance. We use hi-pitched tones to break up the cancer cells' ability to communicate, but there are still some "hangers-on." As Jodi visualizes these cells, they take the shape of a teenager saying, "What's the use? It doesn't come out right no matter how hard I try."

It takes me a lot of soul searching to make the connection that this was how I felt in high school toward the nun who was vice-principal of my small Catholic girls' school. She wielded a lot of power and was able to keep me out of choir, class office, cheer leading and debate tournaments. It seems that she did her best to silence me whenever possible. As I reflect back, I am aware of a deep sadness, feelings of rejection, injustice and failure that I did not recognize at the time. This affected my beliefs and attitude toward myself and my classmates as well. I know, now, that I put up a pretty sturdy shell to protect against further hurt and rejection. All of this needs to be explored and released through journaling, prayer and meditation because this negativity is feeding the sensitive cancer cells in the breast.

   As I work to process this new information, I come up against a question with which I struggle over and over: "Is the cancer real or not real?" Of course, it is real in the physical world where we live separated from God and our heavenly home. But that is an illusion. We are never truly separated from God. In unity with God there is only perfection-no illness, pain or imperfection of any sort. Therefore illness is only a result of our imagined separation from God. When we unite with the Divine and realize that we are the manifestation of God, all is well. I'm working on it!

Pele's Presence: May 11, 2006

9   ✡   *From Fear to Forgiveness*

"Vulnerability, then is not only a product of the wholeness that results from the process of forgiveness; it is also a means to facilitate it and, even more importantly, a way to obviate the need for the process by preventing hurts from beginning."
-*The Process of Forgiveness* by William A. Meninger (p. 149)-

An energy session with Catherine Morgan the following Wednesday reinforces the work I did with Jodi. Catherine says that neuropeptides in the breast tissue cells continue to hold painful emotions related to negative beliefs about self. Fear related to this perceived rejection and loneliness is the message of the cancer that needs to be worked through.

Catherine sees the negative energy of that high school vice-principal stuck in my brain. She/it refuses to be released to the light. After intensive, but futile, work to send her away, I resort to a symbolic funeral in which I bury her, bless her, and plant a sweet-scented yellow flower to guide her to the light. This does the trick!

However, I still have much "inner work" to do. I take out my journal and dialogue with each emotion as to its needs and beliefs and empathize with the child parts who were fearful, felt rejected and responded with anger. I try to go back to my earliest memories.

My fearful child emerged at age 4 ½ when my mother left our seaside home to have a lung removed. The doctors filled her lung cavity with donated blood to which she developed an allergic reaction. She remained bed-ridden with a severe depression for 2-3 months. I did my best to help our exhausted father care for my 3 year old sister, Terri, and the 6 month old twins, Sally and Sandra, but was really not up to the task. I struggled with feelings of loneliness and abandonment. My fearful four year old self needs reassurance and the knowledge that she has never been alone, never been separated from God and has, in fact, always been surrounded by angels and heavenly guides. Feelings of aloneness and separation and being overwhelmed were all illusion. Reality is one of continual support by God and the angels and a benign universe that wishes her well.

The next step of this process is to bring the element of forgiveness into the picture:

- Forgiveness for the self that allowed this false sense of separation to exist for so long.

- Forgiveness for the situation (my parents' physical illness and emotional wounds) that prevented needed comfort, dialogue and reassurance.

- Forgiveness for family members who didn't come forward to help my parents, for the world situation (the economic

"Depression" and WWII that caused my father's asthma) which compounded our family's difficult situation.

- Forgiveness for those who caused this situation through ignorance, greed and/or abuse of power.

- Forgiveness for church officials who laid burdens on married couples and offered little support and lots of condemnation.

Only after I exhaust the reaches of my need to forgive am I able to return and give great thanks to the kind neighbors, friends and dedicated doctor who went way beyond traditional caring to support our little family through an incredibly difficult time.

Next I address that part of myself that felt rejected and believed she wasn't wanted, liked or appreciated. I am aware of harboring some of these thoughts and feelings as a child whose chores or performance never quite met the expectations of a perfectionist mother. But there was always lots of praise to offset the criticism.

By far the biggest wounds in this area were inflicted in high school. After forgiving all involved, as well as myself for not being able to speak my own truth, I am finally able to move on to giving thanks for the good things that helped shape me into the person I am now. There were many successes, both in school and in my numerous 4-H activities, which helped me become competent and self-confident. However, one great gift was given to me on graduation day by our music director, Mrs. Ellis, who let me know that she thought I had a good singing voice and had always wanted me in choir, but that a certain nun had kept me out. This confirmed my suspicions that many of my failures to accomplish school-related goals had little to do with personal inadequacies. Her comments freed me from beliefs that I was not good enough and that my classmates didn't like me.

The most difficult part of self for me to work with was the angry child. This huge anger grew out of a sense of not being acknowledged, listened to or appreciated. I felt that I did not have the power to make my wishes, needs, wants and ideas known. This was sometimes true as a child when my parents struggled with health and financial concerns and had little energy left to focus on their daughter's emotional welfare. It was certainly true in Catholic school when one nun in a classroom of fifty children ruled with an iron fist and tolerated little "personal expression." Even when I found ways to speak up as I grew older, it seemed my ideas were often discounted simply because I was a woman.

I am most grateful for my parents, who encouraged me to join 4-H and Scouts, and for the many dedicated leaders and extension agents who encouraged my talents and leadership skills. It was in these arenas that I began to claim my voice and express my unique gifts and creativity. This remains somewhat of a challenge for me as I continue to struggle to speak up to John regarding my needs and wishes, especially when they conflict with his. However, he continues to try to respond graciously.

I know that this anger stems from fear of not being heard and this is all an illusion because God not only hears, but anticipates my every want and need. These fears are all rooted in my deepest need: to know that we are one, that any sense of separation is an illusion on my part. So, at all times, I am heard, affirmed and deeply loved and appreciated by God, my angels and guides who are always at my beck and call. I continue to work at forgiving myself and anyone who led me to believe otherwise. I give unending thanks to my angels and guides for the gifts and faithful service throughout my lifetime, and especially during these past few weeks.

The Illusion of Control

The following week I meet with Janna Moll, my Healing Touch supervisor and a highly intuitive energy worker. I do further work on positive visualization and associations for healing the breast. I also strengthen my resolve to join my will with God's and claim my ability to let Spirit work through me as a gifted healer. I invite the support of the angels as I step into this power, claim these gifts and release all fears that bind me. I become more aware of my need to release efforts at control and trust the process, leaving the outcome to God.

It's becoming more obvious that this breast cancer has multiple messages for me. It is definitely about letting go of control and trusting in the Lord. It is also very much about nurturing, crying unshed tears of both sadness and joy, claiming the sweetness of life (no need for sugar), releasing both negative emotions and the negative thoughts that accompany them and, finally, claiming my own personal relation with the Divine.

I am again reminded by Fr. Keating (via video) of the need to let go of all need to control, recognize that all feelings are temporary, thus not to be resisted or clung to, and that we can never know with certitude. Again these lower three chakra challenges rear their formidable heads. As Fr. Keating reminds us repeatedly, these three emotional programs for happiness are misbegotten and lead only to pain. I reread *Invitation to Love*, Thomas Keating's book on Christian contemplation published in 1992. He says exactly what Janna told me on Monday: look at the attempt to control and stop doing it. "When asked for advice, say 'this or that.' Listen more; talk less, and make fewer choices. Be open to spirit!" Curing cancer is going to be a piece of cake compared to mastering this saintly man's directives.

Throughout this month I have continued to see clients and attend the usual meetings and social affairs. My one major concession to the cancer (besides hydration, diet, exercise, prayer, meditation and all this introspection and letting go) is to try to get a good eight hours of sleep per night. My energy remains high, but I feel a real need to "get away from it all."

The perfect opportunity arises when a friend we met at our last Healing Touch anatomy class invites Franny and myself to visit her in the tiny mountain town of Twin Lakes. This is definitely a little piece of heaven on earth. Franny, Cornelia and I share meditations from the shamanic journey, relax to the sound healing CD, visit friends, walk in the woods, sit in the sun by a waterfall and enjoy light, healthy organic meals together. Our twenty-four hour getaway is as refreshing as a week long retreat.

Upon returning to Denver I feel energized by our brief mountain expedition and tackle a few of the projects I've been putting off all month. My biggest project is to get my business, which I incorporated last year under the name *Heart's Connection*, squared away with the state and federal government regarding unemployment insurance and various taxes that I naively thought I wouldn't have to worry about as sole employee/owner. After catching up on paperwork, as well as, ironing and mending and having the carpets cleaned, I feel like a new person. I really find it hard to focus when I'm distracted by clutter, loose ends and missed deadlines.

I go to get a baseline Thermogram and am disappointed when it shows a large cancerous mass still present in my right breast. It's not yet been six weeks since diagnosis, but I've worked so hard and have such good energy that I was hoping it would just, miraculously, be gone.

John and I enjoy a lovely weekend of dancing and dining. David's friends invite us to a barbecue celebrating his 25th birthday. We meet with two couples from Spokane who also graduated from Gonzaga. One of the women, a nurse, whom I haven't seen since college, "just happened to have" a video by a female doctor who used diet and prayer to cure a very aggressive breast cancer. Dr Lorraine Day, M.D. corroborates everything I have been doing, and her story of struggle, pain and eventual success gives me the confidence I need to hang in there despite the disappointing thermogram.

Throughout this second week in June I continue to get positive messages from the angels as well as from the various women who I am seeing for Healing Touch and other energy sessions. The morning of June 15th, which is actually David's 25th birthday and exactly six weeks from the date of my diagnosis, I awake at 2 a.m. with certainty that I have turned the corner. I know the cancer is shrinking, and I have won this battle. It will still be some time before I am completely cancer free, but I am ready to celebrate. I take my crystals, Willow Tree angels and angel cards outside, form a healing circle and give thanks for all the help I've received in achieving this victory.

Later that day our son, Michael, and daughter, Carrie, and her family arrive from California to celebrate David's birthday and Father's Day. My positive attitude is contagious. We all have a great time together on this beautiful weekend. The yard looks lovely even though the rabbits, that have made a home beneath ours, have devastated the vegetable garden. We play ball and card games, swim and visit our fabulous Denver zoo. These four days fly by.

Everyone in my family is relieved that I appear healthy and happy, but they are also worried about my decision to spend a week with my youngest sister, Sandy, as she recovers from hip-replacement surgery. I give lots of reassurance that I will continue to take good care of myself.

Prior to leaving for Sandy's house in Eugene, OR, I meet with my surgeon. She examines me and says she sees no reason why I can't postpone the follow-up MRI one week until I return.

On Wednesday I attend our monthly Healing Touch support group meeting where I learn about tonglen. This is a method for working with, rather than denying or rejecting, pain by opening up the energetic heart. I am struck by this image and order a book and CDs by Pema Chodrin, who teaches this powerful form of forgiveness, acceptance and loving-kindness.

As part of our group sharing, we each draw an archetype card and discuss its meaning for us. I draw the "Scribe" with encouragement to write and the warning not to embellish the truth. I began writing the story of how I got involved in Healing Touch this past spring, but have not written anything, except daily journal entries, for the past two months. The thought crosses my mind that, once I overcome this cancer, I will have a different story to tell. For the present, I am trying to live in the moment rather than too far in the future. I recall that, if we can't be "here now," we are "nowhere."

A Week in Oregon

In preparation for my week's trip, I visit Dr. Conrardy, who aligns my spine and balances my energy fields so that I will be able to stay centered in self care but also open to my sister's pain. During a phone call Gina reminds me that this is a time to rise above past hurt and fear and see myself differently. I work with that message for awhile. Does that mean that I could benefit from re-examining my roles as wife, mother, sister, teacher, therapist, healer? Perhaps it means that I need to repair some relationships. Or maybe I need to look with a new eye at my gifts and talents and refocus. Anyway I look at this message, it seems to mean change, letting go, moving on. Each day of these past few weeks I am reminded that life is a journey; we can view it as perilous and drag our feet or as exciting, and dance. I'd rather dance.

Though I've lived in Denver for thirty years, returning to Oregon where I was born, always feels like "going home." Sandy is still in the hospital and anxious to be released when I arrive. The surgery went well; she is making a good recovery. High on Demerol, she's not sure she'll "really need me", but will enjoy the company. Things look a bit different when she gets home. There's a lot to learn about self-care and physical limitations after a hip-replacement.

Fortunately, Sandy is a quick study. Within two days she is on an effective medication schedule, has figured out how to shower and dress with minimal assistance, and the strength and mobility of her leg has increased rapidly. A cold compress machine, generously loaned to her by a new neighbor, greatly accelerates her recovery by reducing pain and swelling.

We have a great time together, sharing childhood memories and reminiscing about events in high school and college days and summer visits when our children were small. We also eat well from the prolific garden she managed to plant prior to surgery, share favorites from our book club selections and laugh a lot. By the time I am ready to leave, she is walking with ease and helping me weed her garden. This has been a wonderful week of love and appreciation experienced by two sisters whose recent lives have taken them in different directions. I am so glad I have been able to spend this special time with her.

After returning from Oregon, I go for a second MRI which shows that the area of the cancer is down from 6x4x2cm to 4x3x.5cm. I am encouraged, but my surgeon cautions me that this reduction could be due to reduced swelling from the biopsies which were done just prior to my first MRI. The mass is still too large for a lumpectomy, and she again recommends a mastectomy. I sign a waiver and say that I have more to learn about myself and this cancer before I can agree to surgery. I promise to see her in two months and call if ever I notice anything of concern.

Unfortunately, John communicates the news to our children and his family by telling them I am "in remission". Two weeks pass before I discover this, and it is very difficult trying to set the record straight. We have some long, heartfelt talks about his fears and my need to be in charge of my own healing and any information shared with respect to that. He agrees and offers total support.

After a fun 4th of July celebration with neighbors I again visit Catherine Morgan, who tells me I need to be using essential oils and taking a more powerful vitamin supplement. On the way home I run into a former neighbor at the grocery store who just happens to be selling a new line of health products. Another serendipitous encounter! Upon contacting a local holistic doctor, I discover that he has recently formulated a special blend of oils for a friend who has cancer. He offers me a small vial.

Several Healing Touch companions and I take a day off to visit a wonderful rock shop in the beautiful mountain town of Nederland where I add to my collection of crystals. With John gone for a few days, I enjoy a funny popular movie with friends and then sit in meditation, surrounded by my healing crystals, trying to make sense of this journey.

I believe that I am healing on the upper levels of my field and that soon this will manifest physically in my breast. I have no idea how long this will take. I know that I have much more to learn about the heart's being intelligent in a different way than the brain. I'm still struggling to learn how and when to use one over the other and to balance my masculine and feminine energies. I am currently reading, journaling and meditating more on both **forgiveness** and **kindness**. I am working on "rejecting" unhealthy cells and "attracting" healthy ones.

July 14th is Michael's 35th birthday, so I meet with Catherine to give him a gift of long distance energy. Unfortunately he experiences it as a "bolt from the blue." His leg gives out on the 9th hole at the Torrey Pines golf course, and he spends the rest of his birthday icing his knee. Perhaps I need to be more specific in how my energy gifts are delivered.

Unheeded Warning

A few days later I returned for a second Archetypal reading with Janna Moll. Janna had foreseen a health crisis in my reading this past January, but I chose to interpret it as referring to the residual effects of the Bells Palsy. This current reading is more positive and indicates that I am moving successfully through much transition. I am encouraged to delve deep to see inner truth, tell my story and write. There are a few warnings, mostly about clearing out clutter, letting go of "busyness" and making time to be quiet so I can see clearly. A lengthy retreat is suggested. This has also been suggested by my chiropractor and massage therapist, and I have set time aside in September. Once again I fail to heed these archetypal messages in a timely manner.

As is typical, my counseling/Healing Touch practice has slowed during these summer months, but the work I am doing with clients often seems more intense and effective. In my personal life I am working on "acceptance" and letting go of judgment. I have also seen a chiropractor who works to clear pathogens from all systems of the body. I am hoping to release any old viruses that may be hanging around from the initial attack of Bells Palsy that might be hindering the full recovery of the facial nerve.

On July 23rd John and I drive south to Durango where we meet our children and grandchildren for a week at the Wilderness Trails Dude Ranch. I learned to ride as a kid from my aunt and uncle who trained horses, and I have really been looking forward to this adventure and sharing my love of horses with the rest of my family. Everyone is having a great time; we've danced, hiked and ridden every day when, without warning, my horse, Colonel, jumps off the trail, digs in his heels, and I land on my rear with a thump. Fortunately I avoid the numerous rocks and, after a massage and some Advil, I'm as good as new.

To my consternation, the exact same scenario is repeated on Friday during our final ride. Again, I avoid serious injury, but displace a lower left rib, which is quite painful. Neither my massage therapist nor chiropractor can get it to go in. Three people had told me I needed to slow down and go away on retreat for a week. I had resisted this good advice, but this horse has forced me to do just that. It's hard to do much with a displaced rib.

I am still in distress two weeks later when I drive to the annual Healing Touch conference in Breckenridge, so I sign up for a session with a medical intuitive. She tells me that the displaced rib represents the torsion in my body: my upper body is twisting and reaching for the light, willing to surrender to God, while my lower body is planted firmly on the earth, unwilling or unable to trust enough to make this leap of faith, still struggling with issues of fear and judgment. The rib at T-7 is the place where the solar plexus (3rd chakra representing will power and self esteem) meets the heart (4th chakra governing relationships). I need to release the lower chakras into God's loving embrace so that this rib can return to its proper place where it can support and protect the heart. Pain is the nudge I need to accomplish this needed change in perception. I am most definitely ready to do the work necessary to be free of this pain.

Early in the morning, one of our roommates, a loving and gracious nun, has a dream of my falling into her arms. I interpret this to mean that I can let go, become untwisted and be supported by the arms of a loving God. The following week I go to a conference where I find a book titled *Falling into the Arms of God*. It is the story of Teresa of Avila's journey to God with an emphasis on the theme of "surrender." As soon as I begin reading this book, my rib goes back in place.

10   *The Hard Work of Surrender*

Kabir says: Student, what is God?
He is the breath inside the breath.

> – quoted by Robert Bly in
> *The Soul is Here for Its Own Joy-*

On August 14th, I have a third two hour session with Jodi Reed. The emphasis is on looking at my sorrow over the many struggles my children have endured and my grief of feeling so powerless in the face of it all. I work to replace the grief with love, and Jody sees the cancer cells break up. I feel significantly "lighter" after this session and have a slightly upset stomach for a couple of days as I work to digest this new way of looking at things and all this released emotional content.

I have spent much of this month reading a book on healing by Cyndi Dale. She describes four pathways of healing. I am following the pathways that require physical changes regarding diet, rest and exercise as well as emotional release and a change in thinking. But the Divine Pathway of choosing love over fear is the road I believe will lead to my complete healing. This means I need to let go of any thoughts which interfere with my ability to connect with my true self which is goodness, truth and beauty-the place where spirit lives. Again I am reminded that healing requires surrendering to God's perfect love.

2nd Thermogram: 9-7-06

This second thermogram indicates less heat in the cancerous right breast and a doubling in size of the healthy dark blue color. The doctor who reads the scan suggests a six month follow-up. My own doctor says that my breasts are no longer cystic (a problem of recent years), and she believes healing is occurring. Inner guidance tells me it will take nine more months to clear this cancerous mass, but I'm very relieved that it is not growing and that the unhealthy cells have stopped multiplying.

I go back to my "drawing board", which is a list of all the people I know who have been helpful and all the life changes I have made since the initial diagnosis. Through a system of meditation and guidance, I learn that I should continue with the vitamin/mineral supplements, eliminate all refined white products from my diet, eat organic and hormone free food, do regular aerobic and weight-bearing exercises, de-tox weekly and get eight hours of sleep per night.

I do a form of strength testing to determine which products I should use as well as the dosages which will be most beneficial to me. (Strength testing is a system of accessing the body's wisdom by asking it yes/no questions and then using the closed circle of thumb/index finger as a circuit breaker to check the response.) Our bodies always know what is appropriate for us at any given time, and many alternative healthcare providers use this technique to provide the best individual service for their clients.

I also discern a need to keep working part time, go dancing often, meditate twice a day and use my sound healing CDs. When I add to this routine my weekly visits for spinal cleansing and monthly visits to my massage therapist and chiropractor, I realize that self-care requires lots of self-discipline.

I have been guided and invited to take the fifth level of Centering Prayer at the Contemplative Outreach center and join a *Course on Miracles* study group. Fortunately the work of both groups will support the exploration of the shadow side of caregiving, which was the theme of our Healing Touch conference over Labor Day weekend in Breckenridge. I have been studying that idea as described in a recent book by our keynote speaker, Susan Trout.

The topic of the war in Iraq and the increasing use of fear by our government leaders to persuade U.S. citizens to support the war effort as the elections draw near comes up repeatedly in all my study and prayer groups. Opinions vary on the best course of action in Iraq, but we all agree that leadership that could rise above the use of fear as a tool of control would be a blessing. We are all praying for leaders who seek unity and harmony rather than fear and separation.

My daily routine is broken by a delightful visit to a Red Hat club, that wonderful organization which encourages women over fifty to enjoy life and one another. They are easily recognized by the flamboyant way in which they combine red and purple attire. I've been asked to give an interactive talk on Numerology and the Enneagram. It turns out to be a lovely luncheon with the additional surprise of meeting a woman I haven't seen since my wedding day over forty years ago.

September continues to be a month filled with blessings ranging from a rare win by the Rockies to a beautiful night for our downtown Octoberfest, dinner with college friends and good dances and local theater productions. Most amazing is the opportunity to travel by light rail with friends from church to hear the Dalai Lama with his message of love, hope, peace and compassion.

Another Horse Named Colonel: 9-20-06

This Wednesday my former counseling center is sponsoring a day for "Care of the Soul." I've been asked to share personal stories of how I've used Healing Touch energy to support clients through tough psychological transitions.

One of the workshops is offered by a pastoral counselor from Colorado Springs who uses horses to help heal traumatized young people. She has brought two horses: a beautiful black stallion and a mixed breed piebald draft horse. We are invited to sit in a circle, meditate, send and receive messages from the horse with which we feel a connection.

This seems pretty far out to me. Despite my experience with our cat, Spooky, I am not in the habit of conversing with animals. However, upon hearing that the draft horse, Shiloh, had been abused, I send him the thought that I am sorry that such a beautiful creature had been treated so harshly. He turns to face me and, as clear as a bell, I hear "I will never hurt you." This is so weird, because I have no intention of getting near either of these horses.

Their owner begins to tell us more of his history. She knew he needed a new name to begin a new life free of abuse. The name he requested was Shiloh; his original name had been Colonel. Colonel is the name of the horse that threw me twice at the dude ranch.

I finally speak up and tell this story. The owner has me approach Shiloh who, instead of shying away as is his custom, stands quietly as I pet him and stroke his head and neck. The fear I have of riding, which has been with me since that second fall, just fades away. His message is a welcome gift.

Visit with Jean: 9-26-06

It has been many months since my last visit to my former supervisor/ therapist, Jean Clift, when I have a dream that is truly puzzling. I call her, tell her I am using energy to treat breast cancer, and that I would like her help in analyzing a recent dream. Jean loans me a treasured, autographed copy of a book written in 1940 by a pastoral counselor that details connections between physical illness, negative thoughts and emotions. The author links jealousy and a history of injustice with cancer.

I share with Jean the many ways God has appeared to support me in this journey through cancer; then we proceed to analyze my dream. It is a colorless, all white dream in which I use many vehicles to convey an infant to safety. We wonder together where my shadow has gone.

I take Jean's book home, read it cover to cover several times and take numerous notes before returning it two weeks later. I spend many hours forgiving myself and others for perceived injustices and searching the corners of my heart for any grumblings of envy or jealousy. Many of these are old issues. Some have to do with my feeling the need to pick up the slack when my mother was overwhelmed. Others have to do with the impossible situation of expecting one nun to teach fifty students, and the patriarchal system of the hierarchical church, which has a negative affect on the self-esteem of so many girls and women. I try to leave no stone unturned as I explore this need for forgiveness

By October my friend, Franny, with whom I went through Healing Touch certification, and I are expanding our energy work into the outer layers of the field and the higher chakras. As we work to reconnect with our original beauty and purpose before it got distorted by the fears and burdens of human life, the goddess, Pele, sends me another message. Franny receives this visual and auditory message for me in which Pele says, with respect to the cancer, that victory is mine, and that I am stronger than I think. She also says that water is healing. I can benefit from swimming with the dolphins because their messages of strength, freedom and grace under pressure are ones that I could strengthen in my own life. By the end of this session, the murky yellow color in my energy field, which indicates cloudy thinking, is replaced by a beautiful pastel yellow, and I feel confident and determined.

I am hoping to join John on a business trip to Hawaii in late November. In preparation for swimming with the dolphins I begin swimming twice a week at our athletic club after my regular exercise class.

As the election approaches I begin to get more involved in politics. I attend our local caucus and walk the neighboring precinct with friends, distributing literature for Democratic candidates. I am so hoping for a change of direction for our country. I find it hard to keep the upbeat, positive attitude necessary for healing when the daily news is filled with increasing numbers of dead and maimed military and civilians in Iraq.

My Tree of Life

On October 7th a friend introduces me to psychic, Judy Goodman. We spend a fascinating day with a roomful of followers at a lovely home in Parker learning about how the soul progresses through the levels of heaven from purgatory to divine union. We are also encouraged to take an unbiased look at our life in an attempt to discover our life's contract. Mine seems to be one of forgiveness, self validation and learning to heal myself in order to heal others. The challenge I need to work on to reach these goals is that of self-discipline. I draw a tree with roots, branches and fruit as a visual to remind me of this contract and help me stay focused on my goals.

Franny and I exchange energy treatments again on Tuesday as is our custom. I am told that I am being asked to write my story and that spirit will guide my hand. I began writing about my trip to Peru before the diagnosis of cancer. Since then I have journaled faithfully, but have not worked on a book because I'm not certain of the message. Without knowing the ending, it's sort of hard to write the story. I continue to work on "being in the process" and letting go of the outcome.

The next day I join other women to begin studying *The Course in Miracles.* Gina Fenske had a dream that six of us would read Gary Renard's *The Disappearance of the Universe*, reviewing it chapter by chapter along with *The Course.* We begin by praying that our wills will be aligned with God's will and that of Spirit throughout this endeavor. This plea will become my daily prayer.

The Wounded Healer

One Wednesday evening in October, I present a reflection to my Healing Touch community on "The Shadow of the Wounded Healer." This is an hour long discussion I've led several times based on a class I took one summer at the Jungian Institute near Zurich.

The wounded healer is specifically initiated into the art of healing through some form of personal hardship-anything from an actual physical injury or illness to the loss of all one's earthly possessions. Often, if it is an illness or accident, it will be one for which there is no conventional cure. The wounded healer archetype emerges in your psyche with the demand that you push yourself to a level of inner effort that becomes more a process of transformation than an attempt to heal an illness. If you successfully complete the initiation, you experience an exceptional healing, and a path of service seems to be divinely provided after the healing is complete.

The shadow of the healer archetypes is hubris: claiming that you have the ability to cure others.

We began the evening by listening to the stories of Asklepios, the healer of Epidaurus, made famous by Homer and of Chiron, the mythical half man/half horse whose magical powers could outwit death. He was wounded by a poisoned arrow, freed from his suffering by merciful gods and now reigns in the winter sky as the Archer, Sagittarius. Then we shared our own stories of the wounding that led us into the healing profession and our own run-ins with the dangerous hubris. It was a powerful evening.

I ended the evening with some time honored advice regarding what the wounded healer can do if she is unable to heal herself:

- Let go of control.

- Wash seven times in the River Jordan (this refers to fasting) to remove blocks to God's grace (prayer).

- Excavate for painful, buried emotions, feel the emotions, release negative beliefs and invite in forgiveness.

- Nurture the physical body.

I try hard to follow this excellent advice myself.

"I Say, 'Yes,' My Lord": 10-19-06

Our study group rereads the story of the Prodigal Son. We all relate to the wayward younger son, who squanders his inheritance and comes back begging forgiveness, as well as to the elder "good" son who feels cheated. With this reading we focus on the notion of the prodigal father, who is generous beyond our human concept. He waits patiently, bearing no grudge, until his younger son wakes up and returns home, and then celebrates that return. Surely this is like our heavenly father, who can't wait for us to wake up and come home again. This is a loving God in Whom I can easily place my trust.

On Saturday I attend a Day of Prayer at Our Lady of Lourdes by Benedictine Abbot, Fr. Joseph. His theme is "I say Yes, My Lord"-our unconditional positive response to God. I've been struggling with this theme myself for some time now. Thinking of God as a loving father who can't wait to shower me with an abundance of gifts is helpful. This level of trust in God demands a release of all fear and changing any old patterns of thought that keep one from accepting the unconditional love of God. There are, however, some less than admirable aspects of my personality that I must release before I can truly assent to God's will for me. I am reluctant to let go of the tendency to speak off the top of my head, rather than slow down and come from the heart. I seem to have a bad case of "foot in mouth" disease. I hope it's not incurable.

John and I continue to dance and have even committed to a few lessons. We both agree that we could have avoided some bad habits had we done this many years ago. I notice that, as he becomes a stronger, more confident leader, I can follow more gracefully-another personal lesson in surrender.

.

11 ✡ *Journey to Wholeness*

Wild Nights – Wild Nights!

Wild Nights - Wild Nights!
Were I with thee
Wild Nights should be
Our luxury!

Futile – the Winds –
To a Heart in port –
Done with the Compass –
Done with the Chart!

Rowing in Eden –
Ah, the Sea!
Might I but moor – Tonight –In Thee!

-Emily Dickinson-

An early snow covered the ground at the Jesuits' Sacred Heart Retreat House as I joined forty women from Pax Christi, my parish church, for a weekend retreat. I open the retreat by striking a huge clay pot with a hammer. Our retreat director, Molly Stewart, will lead us through exercises over the next two days for reclaiming these broken pieces of ourselves. One of the women moves us to tears by inviting us to write our brokenness on her body with markers and "wearing our wounds" for the remainder of the day. The healing and deep sharing that result from this openness make this one of the most powerful retreats I have ever attended.

Family Celebrations: 11-06

In early November John and I fly to San Diego to celebrate the first birthday and baptism of our youngest grandson, Ryan. It is a joy to be with all our children, but it's a rough weekend for our daughter, Carrie, who is suffering from the flu, bronchitis and walking pneumonia. It's difficult to find time to do Healing Touch amidst all of this family confusion, but we do our best. Carrie improves enough to join the rest of the family for a special dinner to celebrate John's 65th birthday and an early Thanksgiving.

The children present John with a wonderful scrapbook, a true work of art that Carrie has spent countless hours designing. They also give him an elaborate trophy acknowledging his wins in their fantasy baseball competitions during four of the past six seasons. This annual obsession among the men in our family drives the women slightly nuts-just another lesson in forgiveness and letting go of what we can't control. It's one of many when you are a family that plays together.

The Dragon Stirs

On November 21st I have a second ultrasound which indicates no significant change in the shape of the cancerous mass since detection in May. Given the positive results of the thermogram, I am very disappointed. Both John and my Healing

Touch friends are comforting and supportive. Teachers and mentors encourage me to keep up the good work and continue to surrender to the power of God's light and love. Others suggest I follow my surgeon's advice to remove it. I am feeling very confused.

I have recently begun taking a year long energy-psychology class in Boulder, CO. based on the work of Barbara Brennan. Our class is taught by an intuitive healer, Carolyn Eberle, who offers me the following information:

- She reminds me that I practice the art of surrender whenever I do energy work.

- She guides me in discerning divine intent for myself in this situation.

- She suggests I confront and release any fears about surgery since I will manifest what I attach my energy to.

- She suggests I ask for enlightenment in a dream. (This is especially helpful as that night I do have a dream in which I am fighting my surgeon with all my might.)

- Caroline also acknowledges the hard work I've done on the physical, emotional and mental levels to overcome this cancer. However, she says it is being driven by a powerful force in the unconscious.

This is a very disturbing comment. At first I am angry that she would shake my confidence with such negativity. However, after some consideration, I decide it's best that I know what a powerful adversary I am up against.

I take a break from fretting over the ultrasound results to enjoy a second Thanksgiving dinner with our youngest son, David, his girlfriend, Katie, and her family. We also spend a delightful evening with them at a local production of the Roger and Hammerstein musical, *Cinderella*. Sunday, John and I compose our annual Christmas letter. This year it is a very brief holiday greeting that includes a photo of our entire family seated on horses at the dude ranch, which John has painstakingly manufactured from individual shots using photo shop software. The kids love it. Most don't notice that the two youngest grandsons are riding the same very gentle, very old horse.

On Monday, November 27th I drive again to Louisville to visit Jodi Reed. This time Jodi's guidance leads me to associate with the Blue Fairy in Pinocchio who, if my memory serves me well, told the wooden boy to be honest and true to himself. Jodi guides me in connecting to my true self and in releasing any parts of self that feel needy or lonely.

These are powerful exercises that open and balance the heart chakra and release old fears. The green heart chakra holds the emotion of love and mediates between the lower three chakras representing the body and the upper three of the mind. Jodi also tells me that all my cells are very healthy, including the remaining cancer cells. She suggests taking Chinese herbs for ten weeks to weaken the cancerous cells so that my body can eliminate them.

Jodi is confident that I will be successful in my quest to overcome this cancer, but she reminds me that this is about so much more than my breast. This is a journey of total transformation, and I must therefore venture into the unconscious, or the underworld as it is described in myth.

Fortunately, Contemplative Outreach is hosting a silent retreat this coming weekend at Sacred Heart, and I can't think of a better place to attempt to make contact with my unconscious.

The first weekend in Advent is extremely chilly by Colorado standards, a prelude to the coldest, snowiest winter on record. Though this is a silent retreat we are invited to visit during our first and last meal. When my tablemates discover I am here in an attempt to discern whether or not to submit to surgery for breast cancer, the woman seated next to me says that she happens to have a medal of St. Peregrine in her car. He is the patron of cancer patients. At our next meal she hands me this lovely gift.

Moving toward Surrender

During my session with spiritual director, David Frenette, I learn what is called "The Welcoming Prayer" which is suggested for people facing a serious dilemma or health crisis. This four part prayer includes:

- Scanning the body for physical, emotional and mental sensations and beliefs.

- Inviting God/Holy Spirit into the affected area.

- Releasing all need for approval, security and/or control.

- Asking God to change my heart rather than this specific condition.

I have brought my book *Falling into the Arms of God* and read the chapters on surrendering to God over and over.

At first this notion of surrender feels to me like giving up. However, as David explains it, I am rather to focus on and accept my troubling emotions before releasing them into God's hands. The unconditional loving presence of God is the healing force. By opening to His love I free up energy to deal with the cancer more effectively. I am beginning to distinguish between traditional meditation, which brings clarity of mind, and the release of Centering Prayer, which expands and purifies the heart. It must have been an inspired choice to name my business *Heart's Connection*, because heart work is all I've been doing lately.

On Monday I visit a woman who has a diplomate degree in Chinese medicine. After an initial exam, she prescribes a specific mix of herbs which I will brew into a tea and drink three times a day for the next ten weeks.

I notice two results. Immediately, sweets and junk food seem less appealing. I even manage to bake the traditional Christmas cookies without licking the bowl. The second side effect is that long buried emotions are more accessible. In energy work treatments, I've been retrieving intense emotional reactions related to the fear and sadness I felt as a four year old who thought her mother was dying. The first time I experienced this deep work I had an upset stomach for two days as my body worked to process this emotional release. It's amazing to realize that the cells can capture and retain such strong emotional content for over sixty years.

In early December I again visit my surgeon who asks me what my plans are. I tell her that, given the positive results of the Thermogram (more blue, less heat) I'm disappointed that the ultra sound shows the dimensions of the mass to be unchanged. I have been working to detoxify my entire body, especially the lymphatic system. Since breasts are mostly lymph glands, mine are now less tender and cystic (lumpy) than ever. I tell her that I will be taking Chinese herbs for 2.5 months, followed by other forms of detoxification for another 2.5 months. I expect the cancer to be gone by June. My plan continues to make her uncomfortable, but she wishes me well and says she will authorize another mammogram in February.

I have learned that there is an enzyme, transcriptase, which encourages early cell reproduction. I visualize silencing the cancer cell genes that produce this enzyme and focus on increasing production of Nevirapine, which gums up the process.

Christmas, '06

John makes a hasty trip to Portland to help his parents settle into an assisted living home nearer his sister's family in the town of Forest Grove. He arrives back in time to help host our annual pot-luck dinner for the neighbors. This is always an enjoyable pre-winter opportunity to socialize and find out what's going on in the dozen homes on our cul-de-sac. The next day he flies to D.C. where he is stranded because the Denver airport closes on Wednesday due to one of our worst pre-Christmas blizzards on record.

He arrives home on Saturday, shortly before our children, who struggle over rutted, snow-packed streets in their non-4-wheel-drive rental cars. The sunrise on Christmas Eve day is a glorious pink and gold in a crystal clear blue sky. The children (big and little) turn our backyard into a true winter wonderland with ski and sled runs for the little ones, a charming family of snow people and large, roomy igloo.

Unfortunately, thirteen month old Ryan develops pneumonia. Unable to risk the pressure change, he stays in Denver with his father, Bill, while the rest of us head for an anticipated three days of skiing in the mountains. We manage one day of perfect powder skiing before a second blizzard blasts Denver. Our son, Tony, and his family leave early Thursday and drive straight to the airport where they are lucky to get the last plane out to the Bay area. Mike and David decide to ski another day, while we choose to head back with our daughter and three year old grandson, Johnny. Finding the freeway closed, we detour through Breckenridge over Hoosier Pass. A 90 minute trip becomes a slow, cold six hour drive in blowing snow, but Carrie does a great job of entertaining Johnny, and we arrive safely home by dinner time. A truly memorable Christmas vacation!

Back on Track: 1-1-07

After the children leave I realize I've slipped a bit in my daily routine of self care. I resolve to catch up on my sleep and get back on my hour/day meditation schedule. I am aware of holding on to some anger at a church member who told me after Mass this morning she has read that cancer patients are seeking attention. I release this by swimming twenty-four laps at our local club. I then fall asleep while listening to a tape on forgiveness from "The Journey" program. After taking the Christmas tree down, John and I join David and Katie for a simple dinner, play a few rounds of "Sequence" and call it an early evening.

Forgiveness-the key to healing

Wednesday our *Course in Miracles* study group begins the first of many discussions on forgiveness. This subject has come up repeatedly in my depth psychology and energetic healing sessions. Books on this topic fall off shelves in front of me; I receive ads for workshops and classes on forgiveness, and my angel cards repeatedly remind me of its importance. I even receive a set of tapes in the mail on how to help clients approach this challenge. Forgiveness is following me around like Peter Pan's shadow.

So I wonder: what is forgiveness? Is it offering love first? Letting go of any need for apology? Or is it knowing that I set up this scenario so I could perceive and forgive a shadow part of myself? These are questions I will continue to explore with our study group.

Beautiful Blue

The next day I visit Dr. John Conrardy, a network chiropractor, who also works with energy. He makes gentle, effective adjustments and tells me that cobalt blue, the desired color on Thermograms, is also the color of the fifth layer of the energy field, the blueprint of perfection. My husband takes great delight at helping me visualize healthy "blue boobs." This becomes an ongoing source of amusement that will help offset stress over the coming months. During this first week in January I continue to focus on self-care, seeking balance between my own growth, work with clients and time with John.

Cracking Open, 1-8-07:

It's a cold winter morning when I decide to take advantage of my massage therapist's offer to let me use inert gas tubes to oxygenate my cells, an effective alternative treatment for cancer. To put it mildly, I have a dramatic reaction. I lose my appetite and begin to experience painful adjustment throughout my ribcage. It feels like I am expanding to make room for my heart to expand. Is this what it takes to become a more compassionate person, to put on the heart of Christ? I am reminded again to be careful what I pray for.

Rumi says:

Who makes these changes?
I shoot an arrow right.
It lands left.
I ride after a deer and find myself
chased by a hog.
I plot to get what I want
and end up in prison.
I dig pits to trap others
and fall in.
I should be suspicious
of what I want.
            -translated by Coleman Barks-

Though painful, I believe this treatment opened me up energetically so that I am able to absorb more from my upcoming three day energy psychology class. During our class on "moving energy", I feel significant pain in the facial nerve that was damaged ten years ago. I notice sensations in the area of the left cheekbone, which I haven't felt in years. There also appears to be a lot of angry energy connected to this damaged nerve. I keep discovering that my work is on going. We are reminded in class that, though we are all works in progress, we must remember that we are also each a truly beautiful spirit!

Several of us are spending the weekend at the Zen center near Boulder rather than commute to class in this -15 degree weather and predicted snow storm. On Friday night, snuggled under purple bedding while sleeping in a vibrant orange room, I have a most amazing dream. About 3 a.m. I awake from a spy/murder mystery which I wrote but, in which, I am also the key detective a.k.a. the television show *Mystery Woman.* I have just missed being involved in a murder related to smuggling secrets from a defense plant in Texas via car, train and boat to China.

Now, wide awake, I begin to analyze this dream. Seeing myself in all characters (sleuth, author, murderer and victim), I realize that I have also authored my own story. My mind has created my life, and my ego believes it to be real. I am trying to find out the truth (become conscious). I am all parts of this reality: murderer and victim, antagonist and protagonist in all my life's dramas.

These scenarios are all invented by my true self to help me practice forgiveness, let go of judgment and offer myself unconditional love by forgiving both myself and others. My ego fights against this. It would rather murder me than have me discover the truth that this world is an illusion. When I can let go of anger and judgment, forgive and love myself and others, I will be healed. I will be working on "the secret" divulged in this dream for some time.

The Secret, as anyone who uses the internet now knows, is a book about the Law of Attraction, which says that the thing we put energy into is what we bring into our life. This has certainly been true for me. Unfortunately, I have only been aware of this in retrospect. I am working to become more proactive about the energy I put forth and, therefore, the things I attract.

On Thursday the 18th, after suffering from an uncomfortable case of hemorrhoids for over a week, I again visit Dr. Conrardy. He tells me that the long term benefits of my oxygenation treatment earlier in the month are positive. However, my body is having difficulty coping with the level of detoxification it was forced into. The hemorrhoids are a part of the negative reaction. The cells in my body are all reorganizing and, as a result, I feel very disorganized. (Boy is this true!) I find his insight, chiropractic adjustments and a special ointment all helpful in dealing with this situation.

The sun has begun to shine once again, and I am finally able to maneuver my little aqua Prius through Denver's snowy streets. Meetings are scheduled; my client load picks up; I get to the gym after a month's absence, and John and I go dancing on Friday night.

Our Course in Miracles study group is working on opening up the heart chakra by responding with love and forgiveness to situations in which we might once have felt hurt or anger. I'm also focusing a lot of my energy on working with the dry eye condition that pervades our family. My son, Tony, and grandson, Ryan's eyes are of special concern. I work with friends to send love and light to heal our sad and angry eyes that we might see more clearly.

The last week of January is full of fun, good news and rewarding work. I have an enjoyable two hour visit over tea with

Katherine Claytor to celebrate my most recent thermogram, which shows lots of healthy blue tissue and no red "hot spots". John and I enjoy a perfectly prepared venison meal at a new Italian restaurant near our house before delighting in a local production of *I Love You, You're Perfect, Now Change*. That same weekend we marvel at Helen Mirren's performance in *The Queen*.

Discussions I lead on topics as diverse as myth, the true meaning of Jesus' sayings, forgiveness and fear all go well. Actually, every aspect of my life seems to be in such harmony, that I am expecting really good news when I go for an ultrasound on Tuesday. I am beyond disappointed to find out that there is no significant change in the size of the mass.

This unpleasant news is followed by a phone call from my former clinical supervisor. She is appalled at my choice to defer to alternative treatment for cancer and "lovingly" challenges me to look at my "obvious denial." This call sends me into a real tail spin. I drive to a favorite bookstore for a monthly meeting with my study group and find out it has been cancelled at the last minute. I try to call several friends, but only get voice mail. John is in Portland again, helping his parents get comfortable in their new apartment.

For the first time in months, I feel alone and afraid. I sit in my little Prius in the Tattered Cover parking lot and sob. Finally I go for a long walk, take a thirty minute steam bath and go grocery shopping before returning home. After several hours I realize that the whole ordeal is an opportunity for forgiveness. My former mentor came from a place of love, but also fear and frustration. As a result she committed the counseling 'no, no' of forcing another to the point of resistance. I have done the same. During that phone conversation, I felt like a little girl stubbornly resisting mom's well meant advice! This is not only a great forgiveness opportunity, but it

112

gives me insight into how my kids or clients might sometimes feel when I push my agenda too hard.

Fortunately, our youngest son, David, is coming over this afternoon for a Healing Touch session, after which we will meet Katie for dinner at our favorite sushi restaurant. This helps me refocus and shift my energy to a place of anticipation instead of being stuck in that "poor me" place which is so uncomfortable. I am also looking forward to a relaxing evening of watching two favorite TV shows, *Monk* and *Psych*, while I write Valentines and finish kitchen chair seat covers to match our cheery new window shades. I'm redecorating our kitchen eating space and adjoining family room in sage green and the primary colors of red, blue and yellow. I prefer this new vibrancy over the more subtle colors we've lived with these past fifteen years. We've also replaced our dark-framed windows with picture windows and removed excess furniture and drapes. I really like the more open, airy, brighter look and feel.

Since John is spending the weekend in Portland, I ride the new light rail extension downtown to see the Denver Performing Arts production of King Lear. On Sunday I meet a friend at a well-reviewed opera, which has been effectively translated from the original Italian into English and placed in a turn of the century American setting. It may not be as classy as the recent performance of Mozart's *The Magic Flute* by the New York Met I saw last month, but it is lots of fun.

I am also spending a lot of time reading and studying for the energy psychology class I'm taking in Boulder. Two books I've read this past week, *Listening Hands* and *Hakomi*, both help me understand how to assist my clients in moving the energy related to various thoughts and feelings that get trapped in the cells, muscles and organs of the body. On Thursday, I have an informative chat on

113

the phone with our instructor. Carolyn points out the growth in my ability to follow the energy with clients.

She also mentions that one of my biggest challenges is to let go of the negative agenda of my personality, my tendency to impose my view on others. I possess a strong masculine energy that tends to overpower me and others when I feel stuck or confused. Carolyn suggests I can just let it flow through me rather than hold onto it so tightly. This could be a contributing factor to the cancer. In that case I really need to work at letting go of it, not only so that I'll be a better person and therapist, but so that I can be healed.

I am again reminded that working on surrender means being receptive to the healing power of love. I may carry the archetype of the Amazon warrior, but those women had to sacrifice their right breasts in order to shoot straight. I am choosing not to do this!

This conversation results in my reviewing years of accumulated literature on different personality types. I am an extrovert, intuitive, feeling, goal-oriented (ENFJ) on the Myers-Briggs Inventory and an "8" (assertive type) on the Enneagram. Reviewing the positive and challenging aspects of my personality according to these descriptions is illuminative. All of us on the path of spiritual growth have a need to let go of judgments, comparisons and the need to understand.

"8"s on the Enneagram, who tend to move energy against others, must work especially hard to let go of control and power struggles. Our deeply buried feelings of tenderness and vulnerability are hidden by a lust for power accompanied by lots of energy and vitality. This has been a driving force in my life as long as I can remember. I still have an essay I wrote in high school entitled "I Love Life", which describes the "go for it" attitude I had at age sixteen.

Rereading old notes on character and personality types is a mixed blessing. Being confronted with the shadow side of my personality, that tendency to be arrogant, overbearing and confrontational to the point of intimidating others makes me uncomfortable. On the other hand, I celebrate that part of me which leans toward defending the weak, being the voice for the voiceless. I recall my years as an activist when I marched, organized demonstrations, wrote letters, visited congressmen and gave speeches on behalf of animal rights, the environment and nuclear disarmament. Our society has made some progress in these areas, and I rejoice in having had a small part in raising awareness in my community on these issues.

Though I know I still have difficulty making that heart connection which is always able to relate from a place of empathy, I am making progress in not pushing my agenda on others. I celebrate my lust for life and consciously choose that over a need for power. I've come to own and nurture myself through times of weakness and vulnerability rather than reject that part of myself. Forgiving myself for getting cancer has been a big hurdle for me. I am beginning to learn that strength lies in the courage to recognize and confront illness (or any perceived weakness) rather than denying it. Of course, I still have the option of cutting off the cancerous breast, but that does not feel like the right choice for me at this time.

I am sensing that this cancer is a messenger, and it has something to teach me. I believe that surrendering to the wisdom of the body, versus fighting against it, will afford me my best chance to heal. My good friend, Maria, suggests that this breast cancer is a friendly messenger, which is staying with me as a gentle, benign reminder until I am able to make the necessary transformation.

I like her interpretation. I continue to appreciate all those who are supporting me in my choice. I couldn't hang in there month after month without their lifting me up. I really believe that one of my goals in this life is to heal myself so that I might be more effective in helping others heal. However, I also honor the wisdom of those who have made different choices for themselves, and I respect the concern they have expressed for me.

Having John gone for an entire week has given me lots of time for journaling and reflection. I enjoy brunch with David and Katie and two pleasant trips to the theater. However, I also receive horrifying news that a former client has committed suicide. John arrives home Sunday evening to find a devastated wife. I curl up in his arms and pour out a ton of sadness and confusion. He assures me that he loved me when we were teenagers, he loves me the way I am now, and he will continue to love me no matter how I change as a result of the cancer. This is only one of many times I've given thanks for my husband's great physical and emotional strength.

During my visit with the surgeon the next morning, I realize that what I really want are words which can convince her that I know what I am doing, and that my goal is in sight. I try to tell her that I am practicing "surrender to God's will" and forgiveness so that I can be healed by divine love. She replies that, personally, while she values both Eastern and Western traditions of healing, as a surgeon, she can only trust what she can see under a microscope. Since the number 13 has come to me repeatedly in dreams and other forms of communication, she gives me until June 1st, (13 months from diagnosis) to schedule a follow-up ultrasound and biopsy, if necessary. I thank her for being so willing to meet me on my own terms despite her obvious concerns for my safety. I agree to an appointment the first week in June.

This was a difficult meeting, so I am happy to head directly to our monthly "Bookies" gathering and meet with friends, some of whom I've known for thirty-five years. We listen to reviews of the best new fiction and non-fiction selections. From there we walk to our local "Egg and I" for a lovely lunch, followed by tea and conversation, lots of sharing and support. Good friends make the joyful times better and the tough times bearable. I bless every one of my wonderful women friends.

Tuesday is a time for rest and quiet meditation as I pray for guidance, while the snow falls yet again. I do wish God would blow it all into the mountains where the resorts welcome it. We're close to beating the record set nearly 100 years ago and even my non-depressed clients are getting depressed. Heck, even some of my friends are suffering from cabin fever, and I, myself, seem to burst into tears for no obvious reason. It's been a long winter and our two snowiest months, March and April, are still two weeks away.

Wednesday morning my little Prius and I once more brave the snowy streets to join the *Course in Miracles* study group at Gina's. Our topic is "Fear and Conflict", a chapter in which I have underlined nearly every sentence. A new member, Chris, upon hearing that I am using alternative methods to heal my cancer, gives me the name and number of a woman in Arvada, who successfully used Chinese herbs to cure breast cancer fourteen years ago. I'm looking forward to meeting her.

Today is Valentine's Day and John arrives home with a beautiful vase of two-toned red roses and the perfect card. It says he is the luckiest man in the world because he married the love of his life and "whatever we do, we do together." This should get me through a few more weeks!

PART V
ENDURING THE ORDEAL

Invictus

Out of the night that covers me,
  Black as the Pit from pole to pole,
I thank whatever gods may be
 for my unconquerable soul.

In the fell clutch of circumstance
 I have not winced nor cried aloud.
Under the bludgeonings of chance
 My head is bloody, but unbowed.

Beyond this place of wrath and tears
 Looms but the horror of the shade,
And yet the menace of the years
 Finds, and shall find me, unafraid.

It matters not how strait the gate,
 How charged with punishments the scroll,
I am the master of my fate:
I am the captain of my soul.

-William E. Henley-

12 *A Fresh Start*

Our Journey Had Advanced

Our journey had advanced,
Our feet were almost come
To that odd fork in being's road,
Eternity by term.

Our pace took sudden awe,
Our feet reluctant led;
Before were cities, but between,
The forest of the dead.

Retreat was out of hope;
Behind, a sealed route,
Eternity's white flag before,
And God at every gate.

-Emily Dickinson-

Meeting Marilyn Purdy for the first time is like a breath of fresh air. Her knowledge and can-do attitude totally recharge me on my quest for healing. Marilyn's surgeon didn't believe that she had cured herself of cancer using herbs fourteen years ago and refused to grant the biopsy she requested. After performing a double mastectomy, he had the tissue biopsied. There was no sign of cancer. Marilyn chose to make it her life's work to support and educate women who are choosing alternative methods of healing cancer, and she is a wealth of knowledge. I learn more about the cause of my cancer and what I can do to cure it in my one hour visit with her than I have learned these past ten months. Marilyn believes that the pathogens which have caused my cancer formed at the time I contracted Bells Palsy when the herpes virus that caused that illness combined with yeast from my Candida. The virus enters the cell, the yeast follows and multiplies, as yeast does, to form a very opportunistic organism that wants to survive at all costs and has the ability to transform itself and return after being subdued or cleared.

I learn that I need a specific enzyme that will bore through the tough outer shell of the cell to reach the vulnerable cancer underneath. Once I find the right enzyme, I will also need something to clear the cancer cells out of my system before they have a chance to regroup. Since cancer is an abnormal protein, when it is broken up it will attach to other cells, sort of like Velcro, unless it is removed quickly. I have an ion-cleanse machine at home, which I use regularly for detoxification. This helps, but the enzymes are critical to the overall success of removing all cancerous cells.

Marilyn and I use strength testing, a simple procedure of yes/no responses used by many alternative practitioners, to see if my body is ready for the pancreatic enzymes which are most effective against cancer. After getting a negative response, I try a number of products and determine that taking olive leaf extract and Xango juice will prepare my body for the enzymes. It feels good to have a plan and someone who can help me track my progress.

That night I pick John up from work, as I will do every day this week, because my Prius needs a new auxiliary battery, which is on three week back order. (My friends tell me that this happened because Mercury went into a three week retrograde on Saturday, which causes electrical interference on earth. I'm not so sure, but it is odd that John's car locks and our garage door opener are also behaving erratically. I hope the computer doesn't crash.) John gets the lion's share of our sushi and sashimi dinner, because I'm so excited about all I learned during my visit with Marilyn that I talk nonstop throughout our meal.

The following day I visit our Contemplative Prayer Center to learn more about the "Welcoming Prayer" and what Fr. Keating has to say regarding letting go of needs for security, approval and control. The theory is that, in asking Jesus to change my heart rather than cure the cancer, I will come to a place of peace where I can release all fear. Then, bringing this new level of awareness of God's all-encompassing love back up through the mental, emotional and physical layers of my field will give me the strength to deal more effectively with life challenges.

I'm beginning to realize what a long way I have to go to become proficient at this form of meditation called Centering Prayer. Fortunately, neither God nor healing requires proficiency-merely consistency. I'm reminded of a line from the *Course in Miracles* that says turning our needs over to God is our gift to him. I find this to be a comforting thought, and decide to practice it often.

I continue to receive interesting information throughout the remainder of the week. Franny tells me, during a Healing Touch session, that she sees me recovering and writing a book about the journey. Another of my mentors says she believes I am forging a new path for all women with breast cancer by encouraging the exploration of both allopathic and alternative means of treatment. Dr. Conrardy tells me, without knowing about my visit to Marilyn, that my body is asking for a full spectrum of pancreatic enzymes. He doesn't carry them, but thinks I should look into ordering them.

Two days later my PCP calls to say that she has been spending a lot of time exploring the newest developments in treating cancer since her sister was recently diagnosed. She mentions that pancreatic enzymes are thought to be effective anti-carcinogens because they are produced by the pancreas when a woman is five months pregnant to stop the placenta from growing at such a rapid rate. I love it when information is confirmed, not once, but twice. God has been very good to this "doubting Thomas" throughout the entire course of this journey.

After attending my former client's funeral, I join my therapists' study group where I get lots of support, not only for having lost a client in such a tragic way, but also for my ongoing battle again cancer. These other therapists see me as strong and realistic; not one suggests that I might be in denial.

Friday is a day for reconnecting with friends, now scattered throughout the state, whom I first met when we moved to Denver thirty-five years ago. I am again surrounded by loving concern and heartfelt support. My friends comment on my courage, which surprises me. Given that the other option to alternative healing is surgery and radiation, with accompanying scarring and poisoning, I view myself as more on the determined or stubborn side and definitely, pain-avoidant. This weekend John and I celebrate friends' fiftieth wedding anniversary. What a wonderful landmark. We have only seven years to go!

I spend the last week of February with Carrie and her boys in La Jolla while her husband, Bill, joins friends for an annual ski trip to Canada. Johnny, at 31/2 years, is constantly on the go and keeps my daughter on her toes. Ryan, at fifteen months, is his usual good-natured self despite the discomfort of cutting his eyeteeth. The boys sleep through the night while I am there, and Carrie catches up on some shut-eye. I have a lot of empathy for her as I watch her interact with these two very energetic boys. I remember how tired I often was when she and Tony were this age. Carrie is older than I was at that time; fortunately, she works hard to stay strong and healthy.

Immediately upon my return to Denver, I drive to Boulder for our third energy-psychology weekend class. We are working with the energies of different personalities. I am more comfortable with this information and language which tends toward the jargon of psychology rather than pure energy. I am starting to understand that what I "know" equates with what Carolyn is "seeing" and my comfort level and confidence increase accordingly. I still don't see auras, but seem to pick up similar information from observations and intuition. This weekend we work on a number of techniques to help people shift out of deeply held patterns of grief and anger. I am delighted to find that I can use this new knowledge successfully with clients the following day.

On my way back from Boulder I stop at Marilyn Purdy's where strength testing reveals that I am ready to add two more products to my pharmacopoeia: a protease enzyme and a specific type of acidopholous. I am amazed at how my body uses one product to prepare me for the next and at how I can tap into my body's wisdom to discover the quantity and length of time I need to take each substance. I am also incredibly grateful for the guidance that leads me to the right people at the right time, who can help me discover this.

I am learning what a lot of hard work and determination healing requires, and how very individual this journey of healing cancer is for me. No wonder our medical system is so reluctant to treat us as individuals. It's not just the drug companies that are invested in the "one size fits all" method of treating women with breast cancer. "Cut, burn and poison" is easier than teaching each person week by week to discover what their individual systems need. Individual healing is a labor intensive process that is totally incompatible with the "see as many patients as possible" way our managed health care system is set up.

March, as is often the case here in Denver, comes in like a lion with more snow and lots of wind. Nevertheless, we have our share of sunny days so that tulip and daffodil bulbs send up green shoots poking through intermittent patches of snow. On the warmer, south side of our house, snow drops lift their pretty heads, with crocuses not far behind. Whether it's because of the sunshine and flowers, the enzymes, or the hope I've received from sessions with Marilyn, I now have a welcome burst of energy. I clean closets, order a new couch and meet with my accountant to simplify the bookkeeping details of my energy psychology business that have been overwhelming me. We both wholeheartedly agree that I am the wrong personality type to be keeping on top of all the paperwork required by an "S" corporation. It's an immediate hassle, but a long term relief, to change my status with the IRS.

On Monday, March 12th, I review *Molecules of Emotion* by Candace Pert for my AAUW book club. Dr. Pert is a research neuro-immunologist, who discovered receptors for opiates in the brain. This book comprises highlights of both her research and her personal and professional life. Dr. Pert's thesis is that emotions are stored in the cells of the body where they can cause, not only emotional and mental distress, but also physical disease if they are not adequately processed. It's a lesson I've been learning all too well over these past ten months.

The next day I rejoin the AAUW writers' group from which I took a brief hiatus last spring. I knew that I would be journaling daily as I worked to understand and heal the cancer, and felt I would have insufficient time to put into creative writing. That was true, but it's sure fun to be back with this incredibly talented group of women. Their stories, both biographical and fiction, are alternately funny, poignant and insightful.

Friday, our Tattered Cover study group finishes discussing *Traveling Mercies* by Anne Lamott. We've enjoyed discussing this book so much that closing it is like saying goodbye to an old friend. Fortunately, a new friend awaits us with our next selection - a book of essays by another favorite author, Sue Monk Kidd. How lucky I am to live in an age of easy access to books of all kinds, not only classics and well-researched histories from every culture, but also books that are both entertaining and inspirational.

I recently read Dolores Kearns Goodwin's remarkable biography of Abraham Lincoln, *Team of Rivals*. She describes to what lengths Lincoln went to procure books in order to educate himself on every subject from philosophy to literature to math and science. What an incredibly dedicated man he was, both personally and professionally. Our country has been blessed to have had so many learned and self-disciplined people as founding mothers and fathers. They continue to serve us well as heroes and historical mentors.

The following week our *Course in Miracles* class continues to discuss the necessity of forgiveness, even in the case of horrific events like genocide, nuclear reactor accidents and, closer to home,

9-11 and the Iraqi War, now entering it's fifth year. We remind ourselves that everything in our world is illusion and, in forgiving others, we forgive ourselves, because we are all one. This is easier to do when surrounded by the reflective energy of the group. As individuals, it's far too easy to get caught up in our pain and helplessness.

On a lighter note, I tell the group that I have been rereading Gina's book, *A Delicate Balance*. In it she mentions that her angels and guides, in an attempt to capture her attention, occasionally cause her phone or doorbell to ring in the early morning hours when she is not distracted by her busy lifestyle. My angels and guides must have thought I was complaining about not receiving such special attention because, sure enough, the next morning my phone rings at 4:15 a.m. When I pick up the receiver, there is no one there. I hear only the most beautiful "elevator music." We have call-waiting, which indicates a phone number of all zeroes and an area code not registered in the USA. I am definitely going to be more careful to guard my thoughts and wishes in the future!

Reflections, 3-15-07:

As I look back over these past ten months, I am amazed at how much and in what ways I have changed. My body has gotten increasingly sensitive. I've always had highly developed senses of smell and taste but now, having eliminated most white flour, rice, refined sugar and salt from my diet, I am very sensitive to herbal seasonings and prefer only the freshest fruits and vegetables. The other day I fixed a favorite family recipe that suggested baking chicken in tinfoil. The taste and smell of aluminum in the finished dish was so strong that I could barely eat it, and I had never even noticed a hint of metal before.

Colors seem brighter and my inner sight via the third eye is increasing by leaps and bounds. This began with the Shaman's blessing in Peru two years ago and has continued to develop as I learn to listen to my own body and study with Carolyn Eberle about tracking energy in my own and others' fields.

My hearing became excruciatingly acute after the attack of Bells Palsy, which affects the ear's ability to modulate sound. I also use this sense to become more aware of what's going on in those around me regarding rate of breathing, digestion, circulation, tension, etc.

My sense of touch was also altered after my return from Peru. I am more aware of electrical charges in clients' energy fields and my hands tend to vibrate during energetic interactions.

My sense of intuition with respect to my clients' physical, mental, emotional and spiritual aspects of self is becoming stronger, and I'm learning to trust and follow its lead with increasing confidence as I work. I've noticed some physical discomfort as my ribcage seems to have opened to accommodate the expansion of the heart chakra. Some people describe this process as being in an earthquake. For me, it's more a feeling of being pried open by a crowbar, but I can relate to the earthquake experience.

Something similar happened to me when I was working toward certification as a Healing Touch practitioner. I went to see a young man, who practiced a technique called "Body Talk." I felt as though the table on which I was lying, the room I was in, indeed the entire building, were being shaken to the core. I was wide awake and looked up to see a dark velvet cloth on the ceiling covered by images of my cells, with electrons hopping from one to another as particles in the cells of my body rearranged themselves in response to this form of energy work. I've never felt nor seen anything quite like that since.

Along with the physical changes, have come equally interesting mental, emotional and spiritual changes. As I practice centering prayer and sit in meditation, I notice that I am becoming more aware of my own and others' responses to life events. I am more able to stay in the role of observer and not get so caught up emotionally. When I do experience an intense emotional response, I am able to move back to my core self more quickly and easily. I am learning that initial perceptions are often misleading and am trying to take time to tap into my inner knowing or ask for guidance from the Holy Spirit to access the wisdom of the situation. This usually involves some level of forgiveness toward myself as well as another.

Such forgiveness, as taught by Christ, always says, "I forgive you because I know that in some way I have done, said or failed to do what you just did." Therefore, in forgiving another, I forgive myself and let go of all judgment. I love it when I can actually do this; more often I content myself by recognizing how far I have to go toward the goal of non-judgment. I notice that I am especially critical, nowadays, about the amount of sugar people put in their shopping carts, the desserts we consume and those syrupy lattes to which we've become addicted.

I have nearly three months to go before my next ultrasound in June, and have no idea what lessons continue to await me. However, every day in every way my life continues to get better and better and, I must say, this year's journey has been especially exciting.

The third weekend in March our energy psychology class meets for the fourth time. We work on techniques for helping clients contain intense emotional affect, on building trust and safety, and on energetic methods of filling ourselves and others with unconditional love. On some level, we all deal with early childhood wounding, and we are so exhausted by day's end that we quit an hour early.

That night I have a very strange dream. I dream I can't see well; my vision is very fuzzy. I want to see a different optometrist. (In my dream this man looks like my network chiropractor, Dr. John Conrardy.) I ride my bike to downtown Littleton and find his office. There are six doctors available, but mine is not one of them. I spend so much time looking for him that it begins to get dark. I emerge to find my bike stolen. I begin to walk. There are a lot of people on the street; it resembles a carnival. One man turns on a flare which lights up his mask as I walk by. It is unclear as to whether I have my purse and money or a cell phone to call my husband, John. I can borrow money or a phone, but know I will get home, even if I have to walk ten miles that night.

On Sunday we choose to do energy work with Carolyn's horses. One was abused as a colt, and it is quite fascinating to see "Billy" calm down as he begins to trust us. This skittish animal responds so positively to the loving energy of our group that he begins to nuzzle us and stand contentedly while we scratch and pet him.

As we prepare to leave the stables, I realize that my Prius has a flat tire. Franny changes it with the "donut" spare, which can't be driven over 45 mph. I am mortified at being passed by every other vehicle on the highway, including the senior citizen's van. It is so difficult for me to drive the sixty miles home, with lights flashing, in the slow lane, that I write the trip up for our homework assignment on coping with stress. For months I've been working on welcoming the more vulnerable part of my personality and releasing the need to be in control. This episode would seem to indicate that I have a very long way yet to go.

I can't help but see the parallels to my recent dream. I didn't "see" the road hazard that caused the flat. Being forced to drive slowly certainly causes me to take another look at my progress, or lack thereof, toward reaching my goals of patience and surrender.

The following Tuesday I have an individual session scheduled with Carolyn. This is the first time I have seen her work one on one outside a classroom setting. I am thinking it will be a worthwhile goal to explore any angry energy I might have remaining from the ordeal with Bells Palsy. I don't want this type of energy feeding the cancer, and it would also be nice to be free of anger before John and I leave on a cruise next week.

However, since my 2nd and 4th chakras (emotional centers related to love of self and others) are still so open from working with "Billy", what comes up energetically is sorrow rather than anger. The part of me that comes forth to be healed is the vulnerable four year old, who feels disconnected from her overwhelmed parents and is seeking validation, approval and love. Carolyn relates the value of this vulnerable part of my personality to my dream and my feelings of powerlessness when driving my "wounded" car. She says that my current task is to develop patience and "learn to go slow" with myself and others, especially wounded clients. Since we are all one, there is neither tortoise nor hare, winner nor loser and, thus, no "underdog." Again I am reminded that my strength lies in my willingness to be vulnerable and, therefore, human.

13 ✡ *The Panama Canal*

"...one moment your life is a stone and the next, a star."

- excerpt from *Sunset*, Rainer Maria Rilke-

After I received the cancer diagnosis last spring, John and I reluctantly canceled our long-awaited trip to China, which was scheduled for September. At the time we reasoned that, whether I was recovering from surgery and radiation or having success treating it with diet, rest, energy work and meditation, the demanding trip we had planned would put unnecessary strain on my recovering body. So it was with delight that we discovered college friends were planning a cruise through the Panama Canal.

John and I are both looking forward to this new adventure. We are also reading David McCullough's book, *The Path Between the Seas*. This is a spellbinding account of the twenty year attempt to forge a connection between the Atlantic and Pacific Oceans. The canal was originally begun by the French engineer who is credited with building the Suez Canal. Similarly, he was convinced that he could connect the world's two great oceans by a sea level canal without using locks. He was wrong. Disease, lack of sanitation and enormous engineering challenges cost tens of thousands of lives, and investors lost millions. Though Ferdinand de Lesseps was an impractical dreamer with regard to Panama, I appreciate this quote: "I wait with patience, patience which I assure you requires more force of character than does action." That's definitely how I feel as I await the ultrasound that will indicate the same improvement with respect to my cancer as shown by the thermograms.

Now, as we meet our friends in Ft. Lauderdale, we eagerly await this two week vacation during which our only agenda is to relax, have fun and enjoy one another. As the ship leaves port, the six of us toast each other with champagne, blini and caviar-an elegant and romantic send off.

When John's suitcase failed to arrive before our departure, he made some last minute purchases at a portside nautical shop. Fortunately, he is neither vain, nor a clothes' horse. He uncomplainingly wears the same pair of shorts and one of two shirts during the next three days. His tux is accompanied by a pair of dark blue deck shoes and borrowed socks for our first dinner dance. Miracle of miracles, American Airlines manages to get his suitcase to us at our first stop, Aruba, while we are out sightseeing.

We are all up on deck early to watch our ship be pulled through the locks by cables attached to small engines called mules. The weather is perfect, sunny under crystal clear blue skies, as we join other cruise and cargo ships in crossing 165 square mile Lake Gatun, which separates the locks of the adjoining oceans. We know the terrible price paid by those, who died working on this vast project, and are grateful to the sanitary engineer, Col. Wm. Gorgas, who eradicated the dreaded mosquito that carried yellow fever and malaria. However, at the moment, we are simply immersed in the beauty of our surroundings: bright sun, blue sky, and shimmering water encompassed by a wreath of dark green jungle foliage.

During the remainder of our cruise we enjoy wonderful food, entertainment and the opportunity to dance at several different venues. We visit each port of call to view archeological sites and wander past vendors and shops. By far, our most interesting tour is an all day venture to a coffee plantation in Costa Rica. Our guide is a herpetologist, who shares the ecological ramifications of any question we ask. We become mini experts on the produce of Costa Rica and the problems that large plantation owners cause by killing off non-venomous snakes; this increases the rodent population and gives the two venomous snake species room to expand their territory.

However, the most serious problem caused by the large, foreign run plantations is the pervasive use of chemical sprays. The #1 health problem in Costa Rica today is stomach cancer, which is caused by the runoff from the largest banana and coffee plantations. We come back convinced that we should buy organic, not just for our own health, but to save the lives of our neighbors and that of our planet. I decide that every time I see the produce purchasers at our local market, I will applaud their attempts to increase the selection of organic foods.

A part of the cruise I have not expected to benefit from is the spa facility. I plan to compensate for the abundance of wonderful food by following my sister Sally's advice: always take the stairs! However, I also decide to take advantage of this spa facility which offers free yoga and workout classes, as well as informational sessions on health-related topics. I find out that I am low on thyroid, which is common in those who have cancer. So I begin taking cold water kelp tablets.

The Panama Canal

14 ✡ *Family Time*

I am the one whose love
overcomes you, already with you
when you think to call my name...

> -excerpt from *Briefly It Enter* sand
> *Briefly Speaks* by Jane Kenyon-

As the ship prepares to dock in San Diego on Easter Sunday, we and our friends agree that this time together has been so enjoyable, we ought to have an anniversary party. So we make plans to meet in one year in San Francisco to reminisce, as well as enjoy that beautiful city where we have all lived at different times in our lives. Our son, Michael, picks us up at the dock, and we drive to Carrie and Bill's lovely home overlooking La Jolla cove to watch our youngest grandsons enjoy a raucous Easter egg hunt. Carrie has prepared wonderful goodie baskets for all, and we welcome this opportunity to visit our children and these fast growing little ones.

Upon returning from San Diego, I again consult with Marilyn Purdy to determine which products my body needs at this time to continue its healing process. We also discuss using the Noble gas tubes (similar to those I tried with my massage therapist) to oxygenate my cells. The scalar waves emitted by these tubes are known to kill both bacteria and viruses that can lay dormant deep within the body for years. Using strength testing, we determine the proper length of time for cleansing my lymphatic system using this process (15 minutes at outset).

Clearing and improving lymphatic flow are critical for eradicating breast cancer, since the breasts are full of lymph nodes that tend to get congested when the lymphatic system gets sluggish. This machine charges apathetic cells which tend to attract one another, clumping in unhealthy clusters, rather than repel each other and circulate freely.

The weekend of April 14th is a busy one for both John and me. Our son, Michael, is flying to Denver to look at mountain property with John and David. John is still struggling with the cough he picked up on the cruise which has become bronchitis, but he is looking forward to a few days with two of our sons. Neither of us are as enthusiastic about the idea of a second house in the mountains as are our children, but we're staying open to their input.

I am preparing for the fifth energy psychology class, in which we will study ways to explore, master and transform the emotions of sadness and anger and related sexual energies. This is, as usual, a very interesting weekend. We use varying exercise techniques from yoga and other physical therapies to help one another access and release emotions stored deep in the cells of our bodies. Group interactions tend to trigger old wounds, which we process in class with Carolyn's help or work through on our own. In my case, a classmate seems to go out of her way to take a positive experience I share and turn it into a negative.

Carolyn guides me in breathing through the anger I feel at not being heard and then being criticized for something I didn't do. As class ends on Sunday, I leave feeling somewhat confused and upset that, after all our time together, this classmate is still able to get to me and throw me off balance. At the same time, I am grateful for her presence because I am learning so much more about how I am wired, what triggers me and how to diffuse those triggers than I ever would have learned without these interactions.

Fortunately we spent much of the weekend strengthening what Carolyn calls our "empowered witness." At first I thought this was akin to the "observing ego" or fly-on-the-wall we talk about in psychology. As we worked to raise the vibration of our "witness" and used it to calm our personality and center in our true self, I began to see it in a different light. I now believe it is what Father Keating refers to as the "inner witness," which acts as a conduit between ego and a deeper awareness of self. Episcopalian priest, Cynthia Bourgeault, has a chapter dedicated to the importance of this inner witness in her recent book, *Centering Prayer and Inner Awakening*.

My witness helps me resolve the discomfort from this interpersonal conflict and return to my core self. The tensions of class fade away when we join David and Katie, who have prepared a wonderful meal of barbecued lamb and stuffed potatoes as a send off for Michael. He is returning to San Diego on Monday certain that they have found the "perfect" vacation home for our family.

This week I make use of the lessons learned in class to help clients process effectively, or contain if necessary, the anger and sadness that surface during our sessions. I put a lot of effort into allowing them to set the pace and try to make the kind of contact statements that will help them know I "get it" with my heart as well as my head.

On April 21st, our eldest son, Tony, celebrates his fortieth birthday in San Francisco. We're pleased that both his brothers are able to join him and his friends for this special occasion. Carrie, who can't be with them due to other family commitments, is feeling left out. However she will see Tony in two weeks. It's amazing to me that all four of our children continue to make such an effort to join each other for the major events in their lives. They've been away from home for many years, but still manage to get together for Christmas and Thanksgiving, a week long summer vacation and special birthdays.

John and I feel very blessed that they have been willing to make these commitments for so many years. We know, of course, that as the grandchildren grow and their lives become more involved, things will change. Get-togethers may, of necessity, become less frequent, but the new little personalities developing in our grandchildren will make our visits even richer.

This week John and I spend several hours doing chores and working in the yard to prepare it to survive while we travel during the next three weeks. Saturday I join a small group of energy workers for two hours of meditation, drumming and chanting led by a local shaman at a nearby astrological gift shop. I am warned, during meditation, not to try to fly too far, too fast. One more time I hear the message, "Slow down, take care of yourself, remember who you are." In the evening, John and I enjoy a dynamic production of "1776" at our local theater before making a late night drive to the airport to get Carrie. She, too, wants to check out the houses her brothers are considering for a vacation home. In one month, this idea seems to have taken on a life of its own.

After spending Sunday visiting homes in Winter Park with Carrie and a realtor, we take her back to the airport and drive to visit my nephew, Scott. My sister Terri's oldest son is leaving for a second trip to Iraq to help build an airport runway, and we have no idea how long he will be away from his family. He seems happy to receive our prayers and best wishes, as well as the medal of the archangel Michael, which he adds to those of St. Christopher and Our Lady of Notre Dame. Knowing there is no easy answer for solving the mess in the mid-east, I continue to pray for the miracle that will bring all our young men and women back home.

During the weekend I have two imposing dreams. Saturday night I dream I am riding a motorcycle. Though I am going slowly, I lose my balance, fall and skin my knee. I am bleeding, and several people stop to help. I thank them, but reassure them that I am okay. I get back on the bike, confident that I'll get where I'm going

The second dream also begins with themes of being lost, asking for direction and starting over (heading east at one o'clock). Fellow travelers confirm that I am going in the right direction. Then, somehow, I end up as a teacher in an old convent school. I am repeatedly called down to the scullery where I am told on three different occasions to scour the bowl I failed to clean adequately. I work until there are just two tiny spots left to scour.

I interpret both dreams as positive. They seem to indicate that, though my journey has been slow and painful, and I've sometimes felt as if I've lost my way, in fact, all is well. People have been there for me, God has sent me the necessary guidance when I needed reassurance or a fresh start, and I will reach my goal. In fact, I have only "two little spots" of cancer remaining. I recall a line in *The Hero Journey in Dreams* by Jean and Wallace Clift: "In journeys large and small there is help for the hero who finds the courage to put a hand to the plow, and much of that help can come through dreams." I wonder what I need to do to finish "scouring the bowl" to the satisfaction of the head mistress! No doubt, I'll find out soon enough.

The last weekend in April, Carrie and I spend three days together at Red Mountain Spa in St. George, Utah. This Spa emphasizes an active wellness program that includes daily hikes, aerobics and yoga classes. It also offers the pampering and superb food of more traditional spa/resorts. I've been looking forward to spending these three days with my daughter since she first suggested it last fall as a way to celebrate Mother's Day and my upcoming 65th birthday. Bill is watching their boys for the weekend, and this will be our first time alone together since we went shopping for her wedding dress over five years ago.

Carrie spent a weekend with her girlfriends here, but this is my first visit to the Red Mountain Spa. I am overwhelmed with the beauty of this desert oasis. Everywhere I turn there are five foot tall rose bushes in full bloom, flowering shrubs and welcoming shade trees amidst cactus gardens. The spa is bordered by a black lava field, which sits in stark contrast to the red hills that surround us. There will be a full moon this weekend, which lights the nighttime sky almost as brilliantly as the sunrise that heats up our early morning hikes during these ninety degree days.

There are several mother/daughter duos at the spa this weekend, and we enjoy hiking, swimming and exercise classes with them. On Friday afternoon we explore the land, sign up for hikes and classes, have a deliciously healthy meal and spend a quiet evening talking and reading. Carrie has brought me two books that I really enjoy. Jodi Picault's *Keeping Faith* is a page turner that I finish before the weekend is over. The biography of Madeleine Albright, secretary of state during the Clinton administration, is a wealth of fascinating 'insider' information. I will encourage my book clubs to choose both as discussion books.

Saturday morning we join a 'moderate level' hiking group for a three hour hike through Barrel Cactus Canyon. Carrie's picking up steam at journey's end; I am so relieved to see our van as I crest the final hill. Of course, I have expended a lot of energy chatting with our guide and discussing the pros and cons of breast cancer treatment with fellow hikers, who publish a cancer-awareness newsletter and sell medical equipment. I just love to strike up conversations with strangers. There's always something new waiting to be learned. We return in time for stretch and aerobics classes before lunch. That afternoon we read, nap and swim in preparation for our pre-dinner massages. This is such a rough life! Later, we laugh out loud as we watch *Little Miss Sunshine*.

Unfortunately, Carrie is not feeling well: she has a migraine headache. At first we thought she was just exhausted, but now I'm suspecting altitude sickness. Healing Touch, lots of water and a good night's sleep help, but she's definitely not up for the 'advanced' hike scheduled for the morning. We have a light breakfast together; she returns to our room to rest and read while I go on another 'moderate' hike. This time I enjoy not only the hike, which includes petroglyphs marking rites of passage, but also a wide-ranging conversation with our guide/archeologist on topics as varied as physics and energetic healing, reincarnation and the nature of God. This is turning out to be a much broader spa experience than I had anticipated.

Before I left on the hike, I had invited Carrie to look over the draft of what I had written on this book at that point in time, providing she felt up to it. When I return, I find that she has finished editing all sixty pages with little smiley or sad faces and the inevitable, "So how did you <u>feel</u> about that?" I am not really aware of any feeling-type women on either side of my family tree-just smart, hard-working pioneer-types. I doubt that there were many highly emotional women among my husband's German ancestors, who settled in Russia during the time of Catherine the Great and then immigrated to the U.S. from the Saratov region after the peasant uprising of 1904. However, somehow our genes have combined to produce this incredibly sensitive daughter.

I remember when she asked her dad how he felt when he saw us waving goodbye to him at the airport as he left for Vietnam. He told her that he knew I was smart and capable enough to take care of her and her brother. She persisted with, "But, Dad, how did you feel?" I knew she was pushing him into a whole new territory, inviting him to connect with an unexplored part of himself. I was really proud of her then.

Now I'm feeling more empathy toward John. How did I feel when my boss harassed me; when I had to apply for food stamps because pregnancy kept me from teaching; when I feared my first baby was dying of pneumonia; when my mother said I couldn't come home to deliver Tony as John trained for Vietnam? During those and other stressful times, I simply compartmentalized any uncomfortable feelings and did what I had always done so well. I thought through my options, made plans, got organized and did what I could to make it come out okay. To the extent that I even noticed my feelings, I'm sure I believed that giving in to them would just use up precious energy, which I needed to get through the days ahead.

However, Carrie is inviting me, in fact, urging me, to dredge up those old fears, angers, insecurities and sadness. This is not going to be easy, but I appreciate her input. In fact, I welcome her comments.

She is pushing me toward accomplishing my lifetime goal of connecting my head and my heart.

After this Sunday morning "rest", Carrie is feeling much perkier. We so enjoy our remaining time together that we decide to make this an annual event.

Shortly after returning home, I drive north to Louisville to see intuitive healer, Jodi Reed, for the third time since my cancer diagnosis. I have learned to anticipate the unexpected when meeting Jodi. She's the healer who told me that she's known me as Rose, and that I need to learn to work with equal comfort from both head and heart. She also saw the negative energy of the defeatist teenager in my breast who "never gets it right, no matter how hard he tries." In one session she guided me through the pain, sadness and powerlessness I felt at a time when each of my children were facing major life challenges and when I contracted Bells Palsy. I have no idea what to expect today, but am seeking insight as to how to eliminate the last vestiges of this cancer.

Jodi's assessment is positive and encouraging. She says that the remaining cancer cells are inactive, but there are enough of them to show on my scheduled ultrasound. Because these cells are inactive, my body does not see them as a threat and is not working hard enough to clear them out. She suggests I mark them in some way so to alert the healthy cells and the lymphatic system to pay attention and banish them. As a former teacher, I think of red Xs. Jodi likes the idea of a red marker and suggests I buy a vivid red Gerber daisy and put a few petals in my bra to help focus my energy on the work of clearing the rest of the cancer. I leave our session once again feeling both hopeful and amused, wondering at the way she works.

The following day John and I fly to Pleasanton for our granddaughter, Mia's, first communion. As we check into the

Sheraton, where we frequently stay, I can't help but notice that, instead of the usual vases of cut flowers, the lobby is decorated with huge pots of vivid red Gerber daisies. It is the most amazing sight- red Gerber daisies wherever I turn. Knowing there is no such thing as coincidence, I decide to take advantage of this God-given opportunity, carefully remove one petal and sneak it into my bra.

Our weekend with Tony and his family is pure delight. We watch him coach his high school baseball team on Friday afternoon, followed by an informal dinner with Michael and his 'significant other', Emelie. That night Carrie arrives with Johnny, having left Bill in La Jolla to care for their youngest, Ryan, who has an ear infection. We all gather for 10 a.m. Mass to celebrate with Mia, who looks lovely in a simple ankle length white organza dress, her long brown hair pulled back by a curled organdy bow. It's a beautiful sight to see this very athletic seven year old walk with such grace in her new white patent leather pumps, confident in her beauty and her strength.

Having enjoyed a delicious lunch of tacos and fajitas, the extended family heads for the baseball field to watch Tony coach five year old Joey's team. The hour passes quickly. As we watch these little ones attempt to hit, catch, throw and tag, John and I recall memories of teaching our own four these basic skills.

Saturday evening Mia entertains us all with her improvised first communion celebration dance, which includes lots of acrobatic and karate moves, with occasional contributions from her younger brother. Fortunately, her father captures this creative work of art on video.

Our weekend finale is Sunday morning brunch at a beautiful winery in the Livermore Valley. We celebrate, not only Mia's special day, but also John's and my forty-third wedding anniversary, my birthday, and Mother's Day. Joey and Mia give me a cute statue of a frog doing yoga on a lily pad. My children give me an incredible painting they commissioned by a local artist. It comprises all the colors of the seven chakras from the red of the root at the base of the spine to the purple of the crown, and has a healing hand airbrushed in white, radiating light and energy over the whole painting. It's a powerful addition to my office which all my co-workers and clients appreciate.

The next few days pass quickly as we catch up at work and home before leaving for Portland on Friday. John works long hours reviewing papers, writing proposals and planning conferences for different defense department agencies. I have a light client load this week, but am also hosting my writer's group on Tuesday, meeting with my neighborhood book group on Wednesday and exchanging Healing Touch treatments with Franny on Thursday. My sister, Terri, calls to wish me a happy birthday. She mentions that Gerber daisies were our mother's favorite flower, and that she always gave mom a plant on Mother's Day.

Before we know it, we are on our way to Portland. John has been visiting his parents as often as possible this past year, but I haven't seen them since dad's ninety-third birthday last November. It is difficult to observe the changes. Mom never leaves their apartment, except for doctor's visits, and is often in pain due to arthritis and digestive problems. Dad, who has had some dizzy spells and, possibly, mild stroke, moves slowly, but he does go downstairs to the community dining room for meals. They both have congestive heart failure. The last time I saw them, dad was still doing the grocery shopping and cooking for both of them.

Nevertheless, we all enjoy time together on this Mother's Day weekend. John's sister, Mary, who has been making daily visits to her parents and seeing to their many needs, gets a much needed day off to join her family for a ballgame at Oregon State. Mom, for the very first time, allows me to give her a Healing Touch treatment. Her pain is temporarily relieved, and she sleeps restfully through the night. Sunday she asks me if I can again do "that thing that you do" for her. This was a real joy, and I'm wising that I could have done the same for my own mom when she had cancer in her 80s.

We join dad for meals in the dining room and attend a concert performed by a talented trio of local blue grass musicians. Sunday's menu is elaborate, and the three of us enjoy roasted lamb with all the trimmings. It's good to see dad take pleasure in his meals despite the recurring health problems. John and I return to Denver, happy that we have been able to spend this pleasant weekend with his folks. The following day, David and Katie meet us for dinner and surprise me with another Mother's Day gift: a lovely plant of red Gerber daisies!

15 ✡ *Healing Continued*

"The bee of the heart stays deep in the
flower and cares for no other thing

-Kabir-

The week passes quickly as I tend to the house and garden, see clients and prepare for our next energy psychology class which begins this weekend. The three of us, who carpool to the Zen Center on Friday, pass the time sharing all the positive things that have happened in our personal and professional lives since beginning this class last November. We all feel our health and relationships have improved; my friends have begun new careers, and I am writing a book. We are pretty amazed at the number of ways our lives, and those of our other classmates, have been transformed. This combination of mind/body/energy work is really powerful.

Our class this Friday is focused on trauma and how the various personality types tend to respond in differing ways. Though trauma is one of my therapeutic specialties, I learn a lot about how the body responds to trauma at the cellular level. I also become more aware of how the traumatized person, unable to discriminate effectively between dangerous and benign stimuli, is always at risk of being re-traumatized. We work on one another to heal old trauma and re-pattern the body's response, releasing it from the automatic tendency to fight, flee or freeze, which it may have learned in infancy due to a traumatic birth experience or early separation from mom. This is such intense work that I return home totally exhausted.

Saturday morning I awaken with a slight fever; I'm extremely dizzy and have stomach cramps. A high energy class following so much travel has evidently overwhelmed my own system. When I call Carolyn to tell her I will have to miss class she says she is not surprised because she noticed my energy fading yesterday. I spend nearly the entire day sleeping. Sunday, I wake up feeling fine. Both my energy and appetite have returned full force. My classmates comment on how much perkier I look, and I am able to pick up a lot of what I missed during my much needed day of rest.

The homework for this class is an eye-opening experience for me. My first client this week was abused and criticized throughout her childhood, and she responds well to the trauma interventions we have practiced. The essay we are required to write on how we as therapists, as well as our clients, are able to (or fail to)) stay in the present moment, aligned in body, mind and energy, is thought provoking. However, our third assignment is a real challenge.

We are required to do an hour of exercise which replicates the movements of the fetus "in utero" as well as those of an infant up to and through the developmental stages of crawling. Most of these arm, leg and torso extensions are quite enjoyable, but I am having a difficult time with the sucking motions. Mom did not breast feed any of us girls, and I cannot seem to get this head rocking motion down. It occurs to me that my mom and her siblings, as well as my sisters and I, all have had receding jaws, whereas my children, who were breast fed, have well-aligned teeth and jaws. This may or may not have any cause/effect relationship, but I find it interesting.

Upon further study, I learn that weakness in the sucking reflex is related to the C5 vertebrae and an abnormality in the endocrine cells of the small intestine. C5 is the vertebrae that controls the facial nerve, and these endocrine cells, called Peyers Patches, are a key component of the immune system as well as part of the digestive system. Both are related to my inability to metabolize sugar efficiently, which caused the candida that contributed to the Bells Palsy and subsequent cancer. I believe that, when I was born, my facial nerve was damaged. Is it possible that so much of my life history could have been set in motion at the time of my birth?

This coming week I have few clients, so I schedule some self care appointments for myself, starting with a massage on Monday. Later in the week I meet with Tirza Delfinger, founder of Colorado Thermography Technologies. Tirza uses an extremely sensitive camera that produces much more complete data than I've received from my previous thermograms. I now know that the temperature differential between my breasts is 2.18 degrees. (Healthy breasts vary between 0 and 2 degrees, so I'm slightly over normal.) I also received both color and black and white photos which show the differing vascularity (blood supply) in my breasts. This is all information I can work with.

Though the temperature and blood supply in my right breast have decreased significantly over this past year, I am still considered at moderate risk by the doctor who reads the thermogram results. Tirza gives me a book she co-authored, *Better Breast Health for Life*, with numerous life-giving, inexpensive suggestions for clearing away the remaining cancer cells. I wish I had met her and her camera a year ago!

On Saturday, John and I enjoy dinner and dancing at the fiftieth anniversary party of more friends from church. By the time we reach this milestone, we will have attended enough parties to know exactly how we want to celebrate ours. The month of May goes out in a flurry of graduation and garden parties. A former neighbor takes me to lunch and the lovely Hudson Gardens in Littleton. Katherine Claytor and I revisit the Tea Shoppe and spend two hours at the stunning Denver Botanic Gardens where we were a year ago when I answered my cell phone and discovered I had breast cancer.

The first weekend of June, John and I attend a delightful presentation of *My Fair Lady* at the Mainstreet Theater. The production is meant to resemble a rehearsal in turn of the century London, with the cast chatting-up the audience and some on-stage mishaps. We love every minute of it. The lyrics and performers are beyond fabulous. As always, though, I hate the last scene when Eliza fetches Henry Higgins' slippers. I much prefer the scene in which she throws them at him!

On Monday I visit John Conrardy, who uses a scanner to indicate which spinal vertebrae are reflecting either neurological or muscular stress. There is plenty of muscle tension; but of more concern is the neurological scan which shows three long red spikes jutting from the right side of my cervical vertebrae. As a matter of fact, there is an excess of activity down much of the right side of the spine and no corresponding activity on the left. It is as though I am, quite literally, beside myself. Dr. Conrardy is concerned enough about this imbalance that he encourages me to come to a six hour healing workshop he is giving in a week.

Prior to the workshop, I go for the ultrasound that I promised my surgeon I would schedule for the first week in June. I know from the most recent thermogram that the cancer is not completely gone. I was hoping the recurring number 13 in my dreams meant I would be cancer free by now, but evidently I am meant to focus on the Karmic meaning of 13: discipline and hard work.

That certainly has been an accurate description of my life this past year. I am fortunate to have the same radio-oncologist I had a year ago, when I made the decision to work with complementary therapies. Dr. Kaski seems happy to tell me that this ultrasound shows the mass to be less dense and less prominent than it was in previous scans. She would like to do a mammogram, because the calcifications of ductal cancer show up better. However, the Sally Jobe Center does not have my former mammogram film, so the doctor asks me to return in August for that comparison.

My family is ecstatic that an "approved" technology has confirmed my belief that I am more powerful than this cancer. In other words, where the mind leads, the body follows. Holy men and women throughout history have taught that our thoughts create our reality. Renowned 14th C. Christian mystic, Julian of Norwich, had a mantra, which I have made my own: "All is well, all is well, every manner of thing shall be well."

Curious about the imbalance of energy in my neck, I schedule an appointment with Catherine Morgan to explore what's going on. Catherine works with angels, who guide her to tell me that these red energy spikes indicate that my writing is off center. I need to edit what I have written thus far and make certain that none of my words reflect any anger, regret or resentment. I am to use the symbol of the Star of David, an image for me of balanced masculine and feminine energies, to guide my writing. In that way, this book will convey a positive message of hope and empowerment with truth and clarity.

These red spikes hold the energy of fear that has prevented women from speaking a truth that is contrary to accepted societal, religious, political or traditional medical norms. I am being encouraged to rise above that fear and speak from my heart, sharing the wisdom and knowledge I have gained on this journey about how our bodies are made in such a way that healing is God's will for each of us. This seems like a tall order but, with angelic help, how can I not proceed with enthusiasm? As if to confirm the validity of this decision, I am blessed with a vision of St. Rose of Lima, who hands me a book, a rose and a sword made of gold dust. She offers me her support in speaking truth with love and gives me gifts of safety and freedom from fear.

Prior to this diagnosis of cancer, I can't recall having ever had a vision of any kind. Recently, they've become a rather common occurrence. However, this is different in that St. Rose appears to merge with me and become a part of myself. As I reflect upon and journal about this phenomenon, I come to understand that, in telling this part of my story, I am, in fact, telling a part of her story and that of all women whose life experiences have not been related in <u>his</u>-story.

Further reflection leads me to consider the role that our high school vice-principal plays in my story. As I've described her thus far, she symbolizes arrogance, oppression, a need to control and the abuse/misuse of power. I realize that this, too, is a side of myself, a part of the shadow I have been reluctant to acknowledge, claim and, yes, even love. This thought makes me a little queasy, a bit sick to my stomach. Though I'm uncomfortable with this new awareness, I am relieved to the extent that I know full well, "that which we become aware of no longer has power over us." Having become conscious of these traits at this visceral level, I can now choose to act otherwise.

When I return to Dr. Conrardy following this session with Catherine, a follow up scan of my spine shows that the neurological imbalance has nearly disappeared. He is amazed but, from the way I nearly levitated out of Catherine's healing room, this is exactly what I anticipate. I am also interested to learn that the upset stomach syndrome is a common manifestation of a big shift in energy.

During the remainder of the week, I refocus my energy on self care, taking care to eat well, meditate and exercise every day. As I balance myself and plug my own energy leaks (these are real energetic leaks that can be "stitched up" or cauterized with crystals), I also make time to care for my clients, my house and my yard. I send flowers and balloons to my only remaining aunt, who has Alzheimers and is celebrating her 94th birthday this week. I visit a friend, who is recovering from knee surgery and prepare her for upcoming thyroid surgery. Our neighborhood book club discusses *Molecules of Emotion*. I again review this eye-opening book, and our discussion focuses on the power of love in combating disease.

Thursday, I meet with two good Healing Touch friends, Terry and Muriel, to meditate and exchange energy work. I am especially happy to see both of them because, two days ago, I received word that my nephew, Scott, who is in Iraq, was bitten by a brown recluse spider. These spiders are native to Colorado, and so I know that their poisonous bite is a cause for concern. I have been doing long distance energy work on Scott since I heard the news, and welcome the combined efforts of my friends. We are all relieved to hear that, on that very day, the doctor changed the diagnosis and sent him on the two hour drive back to his base. At least I'm hoping and praying this is a good thing. In a perfect world, all our young men and women, currently in Iraq, would be both healthy and on their way back to the USA.

By the end of the week our carpets have been cleaned, the newly covered chairs are back in place and floral sheer curtains are hung, giving our family room an updated, but cozy, comfortable feel. Just as my body is free of energy leaks, our sprinkler system is also leak-free. I've learned that thirty year old sprinkler systems and landscaping, which includes several very large trees, require a vigilant eye.

The same vigilant eye just sighted yet another rabbit munching in my struggling garden. I have already trapped and transported eight of these furry critters to the open space near a golf course this month alone. Ever since Spooky died three years ago, there has been an ongoing battle of wills between my desire to have abundant flower and vegetable gardens and the rabbits' penchant for eating same. I am trying to find a way to turn this into a win-win situation. More chicken wire perhaps? It's not pretty, but effective.

Friday is David's twenty-sixth birthday. He and Katie have invited us to join a few of their friends for a barbecue. We notice the new planter he has built in the front yard, the freshly painted walls, and all the other nice touches that are turning this first house into an attractive home. We stay just long enough to enjoy some of the birthday feast, which includes steaks, burgers and very tasty buffalo hot dogs. His dad and I are quite proud of our hard-working youngest son.

This weekend is also our seventh energy psychology class. Carolyn teaches us to free ourselves from destructive messages and energetic ways of being in the world that have been passed down through generations in our families and our culture. A belief that is prominent in my family of origin is the belief that strong, intelligent

156

women cannot also be emotionally connected and available to themselves or others.

I feel a real sense of freedom and relief as I work to release this untrue, destructive belief. We also work on healing our nervous systems using energetic techniques to repair damaged cells. I believe this type of work, besides balancing my spinal column, is also ameliorating some of the residual damage from the Bells Palsy. Several of my friends have commented on how my face is becoming softer and more responsive than it was a year ago.

Once again, I find the class homework to be challenging and informative. I write up a healing in which we work to release the energy of the victim archetype. Many of my clients struggle with this issue, since our world as a whole is trying to replace the victim mentality by increasing consciousness around personal responsibility. We are also required to write up a situation that irritates us using a method described by Byron Katie. This process helps us become aware of how we instigate confrontations so that others will mirror our own traits back to us. The goal is to forgive all the players, including ourselves, once again recognizing that we are all one. I find this easier to write about in retrospect, than to do in the moment, but I'm working on it.

As a reward for getting my homework finished in a timely manner, I treat myself and my friend, Pam, to lunch at a lovely nearby restaurant called Annabels. Pam is a pilot for United and flies jumbo jets from Denver to Hawaii. She's also one of the most voracious readers in our book club and has a house that is exquisitely decorated with treasures collected from countries throughout the world, especially Africa. I could write an entire book about this fascinating and generous woman and the strong faith that feeds her zest for life. However, what has most endeared her to me recently is that nearly every week for the past year she has mailed me a clever, cute or funny card to keep my spirits up while I tried to discover my personal path of healing. Talk about a faithful friend! There are no words to say what those cards have meant to me. Our lunch is delightful. We can't decide between the crab sandwich and smoked trout salad, so we each order one and share: our food, our stories and our love and appreciation for one another.

On June 22nd, John and I fly to Portland to visit his parents and attend my nephew, John Robert's wedding to his Japanese fiancee, Akiko. My in-laws have been in failing health for some time, and the doctors expect a recent biopsy to show that Dad has advanced prostrate cancer. Carrie and Bill have brought their boys to visit their great grandparents, as well as to enjoy the wedding festivities. Our Saturday visit is very nice. Dad responds well to Healing Touch, seems to have a little energy boost, and does his exercises with weights. I think he looks good energetically. He is passing blood in his urine, but I think that is to be expected after having ten biopsies of the prostrate.

Sunday morning, as we are leaving our hotel to attend the wedding, John receives a call from his sister, Mary, who is very upset. She and Dad are both in tears, so John drops me off at the Portland White House for the wedding and drives again to Forest Grove to spend the day with his parents.

The wedding is delightful, and we all enjoy a lovely reception, but I miss John. Late that evening we discover that both Carrie's and our flights have been delayed. We take turns helping Carrie and Bill entertain Johnny and Ryan in the airport concourse. I'm sure they are even more relieved than we to finally arrive home. However, that relief is nothing compared to our feelings when we learn that Dad's biopsies all are negative. A huge weight appears to lift from John's shoulders when he hears this good news. We are planning to leave for Hawaii on Saturday to join our children and grandchildren for our annual summer vacation. John's mood shifts from one of anxiety to that of joyful anticipation.

We learn, as we check in with David and Katie, that the plane is overweight. The long runway is closed and, as the Denver temperature climbs into the mid 90s, the amount of weight our plane can lift off with decreases 3,000 lbs. with each increasing degree. We are forced to return to the gate, unload 12,000 lbs. of cargo and refuel. The temperature climbs another four degrees during this time, and take off is looking iffy. Finally our pilot convinces the airport to open the longest runway just long enough for us to get airborne. We all cheer.

We eventually make it to Kauai, claim our delayed luggage, and navigate the detours in the dark (thank goodness for a full moon), to arrive at the beautiful Plantation Gardens on Poipu Beach. Thus begins a wonderful week of enjoying sand, sea and surf, snorkeling, hiking and golf on this island paradise. As always, John and I enjoy watching our children play with the little ones. What a thrill it is to see our grandchildren swim across a pool for the first time, spy a tropical fish or turtle with their snorkel gear or ride a wave on their little boogie boards. This week will undoubtedly rival last summer's stay at the dude ranch for "best vacation yet."

One thing we always make time for, especially while on vacation, is reading. John is a speed reader, who can flip the pages of his spy novels so fast it makes me dizzy. The English teacher in me likes to savor words, so I read more slowly. I enjoy a couple of books in a series of historical novels we are reading about the Pacific Theater during WWII.

More rewarding is a book recommended to our energy psychology class titled *Body, Self, and Soul* by Jack Rosenberg. It describes how to use the body as the vehicle through which we express our being. He views the Body as the physical expression of consciousness, the Self as the individual psychological expression, and the Soul as the expression of our essence as it merges with universal consciousness. Each has its part to play in the transpersonal experience that occurs on our path toward consciousness. Once a person makes a commitment to developing this essence or connection to core self, it starts to unfold, almost as a matter of grace. I believe this is the gift of the Holy Spirit. The degree of nurturance we provide this seed of transformation determines the quality of experience we shall have in this life.

This vacation has certainly been a time of nurturing for me, surrounded as I am by the love of family amidst such incredible natural beauty. One of my more memorable personal ventures occurs when I visit the Tropical Botanical Gardens and am allowed on a sold out tour to the Allenton Plantation, since I am willing to ride in the cab next to the tour guide.

It turns out that our guide, Gary, has worked at the gardens for over thirty years, since beginning as a college intern. He's a passionate environmentalist and botanist with a wealth of knowledge about medicinal plants and research. This is his first day back at work after being on leave in an attempt to recover from bone cancer and radiation burns. He healed the burns with oil from the kukui nut and saved his leg from being amputated by drinking noni and Xango juice from the Thai mangosteen fruit for the past six months. He is surprised when I tell him that my cancer has also decreased significantly since I began drinking Xango juice. We are both excited about the research that many young people are doing in the field of alternative medicine.

On a different note, I am also enjoying two books about the mid-east. In *Three Cups of Tea*, mountain climber, Greg Mortenson describes his efforts to build elementary schools to educate both boys and girls in remote villages of Pakistan and Afghanistan. He's got my vote for the Nobel Peace Prize. It's amazing what wonders one person with an open mind and heart can accomplish where the wealthiest governments in the world have failed so miserably.

Healing Continued

PART VI
REACHING OUT

The Twenty Third Psalm

The Lord is my shepherd; I shall not want.
He maketh me to lie down in green pastures;
He leadeth me beside the still waters.
He restoreth my soul'
He leadeth me in the paths of righteousness for his name's sake.
Yea, though I walk through the valley of the shadow of death,
I will fear no evil: for thou art with me;
Thy rod and thy staff they comfort me.
Thou preparest a table before me in the presence of mine enemies;
Thou anointest my head with oil; my cup runneth over.
Surely goodness and mercy shall follow me all the days of my life,
And I will dwell in the house of the Lord forever.

16 ⬡ *Sharing the Light*

"When it is dark enough – men see the stars"
                                    - Ralph Waldo Emerson-

We fly back to Denver on the red-eye flight from Oahu. Since I find it impossible to sleep on planes, it takes me several days to recover and adjust to the time change. Soon, however, I am back to my daily routine. I'm giving thanks that most of our bunny population has found other homes now that we have screened off our lower deck and replaced the overgrown bushes and ivy with a new patio. I'm in the process of replanting many of the nibbled annuals with flowers the rabbits consider less desirable, lest they return for a mealtime snack.

By the middle of July, I'm back to my usual summer routine: early morning meditation followed by a walk around the neighborhood and an hour of gardening. On Monday and Friday I exercise and swim at our health club, and usually schedule clients mid-week. I notice that, as I progress with my own healing, my client population is presenting with more serious health problems, which all have a powerful, unresolved emotional component. This new dimension of my practice is both challenging and rewarding, and is again forcing me onto a more advanced learning curve as I study more in depth the relationship between emotions and physical illness.

An interesting synchronism occurs today as I receive a letter from an old friend whose path has paralleled mine in many ways. Rosie was a teacher when we met at Oregon State University where our husbands were in graduate school. She eventually pursued a career in social work, whereas I chose psychology. She, too, suffered from a serious chronic illness several years ago, which she cured using alternative therapies, encouraged by her daughter, who practices holistic medicine.

Her letter includes information on a silent weekend retreat that she and other parishioners hosted this past April. Tonight I am going to a planning meeting for our upcoming women's retreat. The title is "Words that Harm/Words that Heal" and the overall theme is about meeting God in the silence. I really enjoy these little synchronistic events. They help me realize how involved God is in my every day activities.

The last Friday of July is our eighth energy psychology class. It focuses on the energetic manifestation of chronic illness and ways to work with these various long term physical and mental conditions. I learn even more about cancer and the issues of "space" that go hand in hand with the diagnosis. How have I let others invade my space? How does my way of being mother, wife, sister or friend keep me from claiming my own space? Why is it so difficult for me to say "No" and have my "No" be heard, honored and respected. Why does saying "No" bring with it all these issues of guilt, selfishness and letting others down? Why did I allow this cancer to invade my space and how do I stop this process? How do I invade the space of others? It appears that "space" is a concept on which I will be reflecting for some time.

Homework for this class requires a write-up of how I have incorporated the energetic techniques learned these past nine months into my practice and how that has changed the way I work with clients. We are also to describe the type of client we want to attract and the market we intend to pursue. A friend, who is a marketing specialist, suggests I target cancer centers to offer support to those recently diagnosed. I'm not certain I want to pursue this avenue, but it is food for thought. I definitely have learned a lot about the support that's available and helpful for someone in this situation.

On Saturday I host a bridal shower for the daughter of a friend who is in our Sisters of the Spirit weekly centering prayer group. Along with the invitations we included a card so each guest could write a blessing or wish for the bride. As each of the 27 guests offers her blessing, she also lights a candle and sets it afloat in a tub of water, which is decorated with flowers, frogs and lily pads. We have "Prince Charming's" photo placed in a frog photo frame. It is all lots of fun and a true blessing to have the bride surrounded by so much loving energy.

In early August, my six month mammogram shows a decided decrease in the calcification in my right breast. This is the continued good news that puts my family and friends at ease and, despite my conviction that this "inner knowing" I'm following is God-given, I'm also very happy to have it validated by medical technology.

Later this week some friends and I meet with a number of women who also work with healing energy. We have all overcome serious illness and now share a common passion: to build and staff a healing center where people could come to experience a wide range of proven complementary therapies. It is amazing how many gifted practitioners are working in the south Denver area and what a wide variety of tools and techniques they are skilled at using.

Several years ago I purchased an ion-cleansing machine that detoxes the body by pulling toxins out through the feet and/or hands. It's very effective for treating allergies, sinus infections, gout, arthritis and digestive problems, to name just a few ailments. More recently I purchased a photo-ion machine which emits scalar waves that destroy bacteria, viruses, yeast and fungi, and is especially effective at cleansing the lymphatic and circulatory systems. Its uses seem endless, but I have been using it primarily to support my lymphatic system in removing cancer cells. I've also used it for clients with respiratory problems and auto-immune diseases. One woman in our group uses a quantum biofeedback machine, which gives clients a printout of the efficiency of the various organs and systems of the body, as well as any nutritional deficits. I can't wait to try it out.

The following day I skip my Friday hike to join a peace service at the cathedral in Colorado Springs. It is a powerful prayer service. The lunch, singing and skits that precede the rally make us feel like we are back in the 60s. However some of us choose not to attend the anti-war demonstration. The energy around "anti" anything is not as good as that around "pro-peace". I suggest to some of the "Sisters Against War" that they would emit a more powerful energy if they changed their name to "Sisters for Peace", but I don't think they appreciate my input.

When John is away on one of his frequent trips to D.C., I often catch a movie at one of our local arts theaters. Tonight I go to see the popular romantic adventure, *Stardust*, with Ann Hathaway and Michelle Pfeiffer. It is delightful! On a higher cultural note, the next day I drive to Central City Opera with Katie and her mother to see the French version of Cinderella. We are all charmed by a perfectly executed performance. The drive up and back is glorious, though we are saddened to see so many acres of pine trees turning the reddish brown that indicates the destructive work of the pine beetle. Recent drought and warmer winters have created the perfect conditions in which this voracious insect thrives. It will take our forests centuries to recover.

One of the more interesting and enjoyable investments I've made lately is hiring a Feng Shui expert to analyze our home. She came out for a second time this week to balance the energy of the house by adding vases of water, metal coins, crystals, stones and dishes of salt. She scans the energy of the house just as I scan the energy of my clients' bodies. After every major adjustment, she checks my pulse to see how it has affected me. It has been amazing to watch her work, but even more remarkable is the fact that both John and I are sleeping much better, my arthritic shoulder is less painful and the number of wonderfully synchronistic events in my life keeps expanding. I feel lucky to have met this talented woman, who has been practicing this art and science for 35 years.

Our daughter, Carrie, and her family have been spending the week with Bill's extended family in Estes Park. When they arrive on Sunday to visit us for a few days, we discover that Ryan, not quite two, has a hair line fracture of the tibia due to a mishap on a slide. His leg is too swollen to cast, so he's in a splint and has to be carried everywhere. Since he weighs 35 lbs., this is a challenge for all of us and he, of course, is very frustrated. The strain of sleepless nights and plans gone awry take their toll on all of us. Birthday celebrations for Bill and four year old Johnny fall a little flat. We hope they will all be in good health when they return for Carrie's college reunion in October.

The last weekend in August John again flies to Oregon to spend a few days with his parents, and I attend a workshop given by Gary Renard, who has written several books explaining *The Course in Miracles*. For someone who has tape recorded conversations of monthly visits with "time travelers", who were Christ's apostles, Gary is amazingly down-to-earth, real and very funny. His message, as always, is that forgiveness of others equals forgiveness of self. That is the path of healing and the eventual union with God's Spirit, which leads us home to heaven.

On Wednesday, I have some unexpected free time due to client cancellations. I've been able to scratch off the "must do today" items on my list and copied all the materials needed for tomorrow's Enneagram presentation. So now I sit, gazing through the picture windows on the south side of our house, reflecting upon the many shades of green in my garden.

It's my very favorite color: energizing at the yellow end of the spectrum and so peaceful in its darker blue hues. The greens in my garden run the gamut from the vivid yellows of background shrubbery and fading iris leaves, through the softer grass green of our extensive lawn and two-toned junipers to the beautiful blue-gray of the Colorado blue spruce that anchors the corner of our lot. A brief shower has left sparkling raindrops on the silvery green leaves of the alternate leaf buddleia and lilac bushes. Fringy fronds of the honey locust dance lightly in the breeze while the maple's branches, burdened by their large five-pointed leaves, sway and bounce with a more awkward rhythm.

Generally, I'd see several squirrels chasing one another across the fence, winging through the tree limbs until they land with a thud on our shingled roof. But this afternoon all is still; not even a robin, chickadee, sparrow, finch or their ever-present noisy cousin, the starling, can be heard. How lucky I am to be surrounded by such a wealth of beauty and to have these grace-filled moments to soak it all in.

Thursday, seven members of our prayer group spend a picture perfect day at a "sister's" mountain home in the foothills. We feast on a delicious "committee" salad, followed by the sweetest watermelon and "to-die-for" cream cheese brownies from our local cookbook favorite, *Colorado Cache*.

After lunch I lead a discussion on our strengths and challenges as highlighted by our Enneagram personality types. We are all surprised to discover that most of us have personalities which have developed from a need to please our mothers. An interesting discussion evolves in which we share our difficulties with conflict, assertiveness, setting boundaries, recognizing our own needs and saying "No" without feeling guilty.

Many women our age seem to be faced with similar issues as they redefine who they are once they've moved beyond "the empty nest" stage of life. It is no surprise to learn that, like myself, most of us did not learn to make self-care a priority until we experienced a serious, personal illness. It does surprise me to learn that some of these women, definitely forces to be reckoned with, have never considered going to a movie, a play or even a restaurant without their husbands. So many have given up so much of their true self due to limiting beliefs of what marriage is or "should be."

We end our day with a gentle hike and dinner at the community dining room. As we head for home, I think we all share a deeper appreciation of the gifts we each bring to this "sisterhood" and the value of our support for one another in our chosen ministries.

The following day I finally get a chance to experience Cindy Galasso's quantum biofeedback machine. This procedure balances my energy field, tells me what organs are under-functioning, what I'm allergic to (boysenberries and almonds), and what vitamins and minerals I'm deficient in (calcium). It also scans for viruses, bacteria, yeast and fungi. I am pleased that it finds no cancer activity. (This was confirmed by an MRI in September.) In ninety minutes, I get so much information about my body that I have to take notes. The machine sends vibrational energy to help the body break up and release stuck cell clusters that are impeding healing. I've already referred one of my clients to Cindy so that we can get as much information as possible to help her recover from a chronic intestinal infection.

Later in the day I drive to Boulder to see a visiting Filipina healer who performs psychic surgery. I scheduled this appointment several weeks ago in the hope that she could remove any remaining cancer. Even though I now believe the cancer to be gone, I decide to keep the appointment. I've always been fascinated by the idea of psychic surgery; it makes sense to cover all the bases, and I have a few other health issues, including some pre-cancerous skin lesions (that Scots/Irish heritage) and mild joint inflammation, which I'd like her to look at. This healer works by pulling congested tissue through the cells of the skin, which she removes using astringent wipes. I experience a gentle confidence and peace in her presence and go away feeling blessed with an increased ability to heal.

I spend a quiet day Saturday as my body adjusts to all the energy work it has just received. After dinner John and I delight in the pre-Broadway production of "The Little Mermaid" staged in Denver's new opera house. The lead is played by a local talent who is the most perfect Ariel imaginable. Though critical reviews have managed to find fault, we are delighted with the entire performance, as is the rest of a very enthusiastic audience.

This is Labor Day weekend, currently celebrated in our country by massive department store sales. We decide to capitalize on these 50% off sales to furnish the house we have purchased in Winter Park. Dave and Katie meet us at a local furniture store where we buy everything we need to outfit this house for the winter rental season. Both house and furnishings are a big investment. However, our children have wanted to invest in mountain property for some time, and all love this particular location. We hope it will be a good investment, but also a fun place for family get-togethers: for skiing in winter and exploring our mountain parks in the summer.

John and I celebrate our good fortune by dancing to a favorite country/western band at a local restaurant. As we compare schedules for the next two months, we wonder how we'll accomplish all our commitments. We know we will by taking it one day at a time. We also resolve to schedule more "do-nothing" days when we can practice the art of being.

That is, however, in the future. This week flies by in a flurry of 'house' activity as we attend to the myriad details of buying our vacation home. On Wednesday, John joins me at the chiropractor's for an overall tune-up in preparation for our trip to Hilton Head. The next day we fly to that South Carolina resort where John has agreed to join me during the annual Healing Touch International convention. Neither of us has ever been to this beautiful part of our country.

While I attend workshops and listen to some of the most interesting and uplifting keynote speeches I've ever heard, John spends his time exploring the island photographing the amazing bird population of egret, heron, storks and pelican. We enjoy our fill of crab at wonderful local restaurants and drive to the colorful old city of Savannah for a trolley tour on Sunday afternoon. Though I am learning a great deal about current research and advances in energetic healing, spending time with John in these pleasant surroundings is equally rewarding. He travels so much for work, that we treasure these extended weekends together.

One of the most interesting workshops I attend is a presentation via video by the physicist, Dr. Valerie Hunt, on how the body heals. She guides us through the steps of this process from the initial absorption of the energy of love by the acupuncture points in the meridians. Then healing energy travels through our pink and white connective tissue (including nail and hair follicles), which is even more sensitive than our nervous system. Thirdly, the atomic system of the body is activated as the nuclei of our cells (neutrons, protons, electrons, etc.) are charged and nourished.

Only then are the sensory nerve endings activated. They wake up the nervous system, which in turn activates the spinal cord and the rest of the body until the brain cells wake up. All this activity oxygenates clusters of "stuck" cells. As these "clumped" cells separate, improved circulation of nourishment and "t" cells promotes faster healing.

Dr. Hunt's research has shown how the scalar wave (two energy waves of equal force which cancel each other upon meeting at a central point) is instrumental in preventing or disrupting the clumping of cells in the circulatory system, which prevents healing. This scalar wave can be emitted by healers' hands, as well as by many machines in use by practitioners of complementary therapies, with powerful results.

17 *Journey's End*

A Psalm of Life

Lives of great men all remind us
 We can make our lives sublime,
And, departing, leave behind us
 Footprints on the sands of time.

Footprints, that perhaps another,
 Sailing o'er life's solemn main,
A forlorn and shipwrecked brother,
 Seeing, shall take heart again.

Let us then be up and doing,
 With a heart for any fate;
Still achieving, still pursuing,
 Learn to labor and to wait.

-Henry Wadsworth Longfellow-

Upon returning to Denver I am aware that I'm operating at a different energy level. More "old stuff" is coming up to be processed with such intensity that I need to turn to Dr. Conrardy and my Healing Touch group for support. The angels are getting more aggressive in encouraging me to work on my book, so this morning I am writing away by 5am. I'm also listening to the final CDs in Caroline Myss' Energy Anatomy series, in which her wisdom is helping me gain clarity regarding some of the questions I've been pondering.

Tuesday is 9/11, which has become a memorable date in American history. I spend time listening to a hand bell concert composed as a memorial to all who died on the fateful day-an annual reminder of our perennial call to forgiveness.

Our monthly study group joins to comment on a quote from Hildegard of Bingen: "God hugs you. You are encircled in the mystery of God." We have all felt this comforting, powerful presence and delight in sharing these experiences with one another. By no coincidence, Sunday's sermon is on "The Prodigal Son," which we prefer to call "The Prodigal Father" because he is so unfailingly generous in his love for his son. I recall writing about a sermon on this gospel story at the beginning of this book, which must indicate that my story has come full circle.

I know my journey is far from over. There is so much yet to learn and teach and do that I believe I will live to be 100. In the near future there is our women's retreat in October, Thanksgiving in California, Christmas vacation at our new home in Winter Park and Spanish classes to take before I join Habitat for Humanity in Costa Rica this coming March. My lust for power and control has morphed into a joyous lust for life.

However, I feel that this particular phase of my life's journey is drawing to a close. I have given birth to a new, healthier me this past year. Physically, I am in near perfect health, though not as strong as I would wish. (I really need to lift those weights more often.) A recent MRI and thermogram both indicate that I am cancer free, and all my caregivers agree that I can safely resume annual checkups. Psychologically, I will have to continue work on letting go and surrendering from a place of love and compassion, but I've come a long way in processing the old, buried gunk, all that anger and sorrow which was trapped in the very cells of my body. Mentally my entire way of looking at life and how healing occurs has changed. Spiritually, I've been so transformed that I cannot even remember what it was like to be that law-abiding, scrupulous, good little Catholic girl I once was.

My God will forever be the Prodigal Father/Mother who stands with open arms, showering all creation with grace throughout this earthly journey, until we choose to return home. I'm so glad my parents chose to name me 'Nancy Ann.' Both words mean "grace," and I have, indeed, been blessed with a grace-filled life.

The reward/ resurrection/ gift/ grail that I found on my travels through my own valley of death is that there is no fear. Fear is simply an illusion designed by the ego to keep us captive. It is not part of God's plan for us. Blessings to those of you who are called on a similar journey. Take the time to learn all you can about your disease, your specific diagnosis and your options for healing. Find people within and outside the traditional medical community who will honor and support your decisions. Blessings on your journey. May you be free of fear. May you grow in consciousness and gratitude. And may each and every one of you continue to be amazed by life!

Journey's End

✡ *Afterword*

     Healing from cancer is, in many ways, similar to how the body recovers from any serious or chronic illness; it requires both rest and restoration. Detoxing, cleansing the cells of anything that is impeding healthy functioning, is key. Detoxing is important on all levels: physical, emotional, mental and spiritual. Following is a synopsis of some of the ways in which I detoxed my body to support its innate ability to heal.

Physical

1. Cancer thrives in an acidic environment. Check your pH and alkalinize it (raise it above 7).

- Add coral calcium to distilled water and drink 8 glasses/day. (To order coral calcium call 1-800-7665-0140. Approximately $40/mo. supply.)

- A meat-based diet is acidic. Switch to wild caught fish and natural chicken.

- Johns Hopkins' website suggests an alkalinizing diet of 80% fresh veggies and juice, whole grains, seeds, nuts, cooked beans and a small amount of fresh fruit to provide the enzymes to build healthy cells and strengthen the immune system.

2. Eliminate white foods.

- Sugar feeds cancer-eliminate it and all artificial substitutes made from chemicals. Use raw honey, molasses or fruit juice, if necessary.

- Table salt is bleached. Use sea salt, Bragg's aminos or herbs.

- Avoid milk. It causes mucus in the digestive tract which fuels cancer. Try unsweetened soy, rice or coconut milk.

- Substitute brown rice for white and whole wheat or multi-grains for white flour.

3. Avoid alcohol (sugar) and caffeine (stimulants).

4. Exercise regularly: both aerobic and weight-bearing. Yoga and swimming are especially recommended.

5. Sleep 8 hours/night. The most restorative sleep occurs between 10 & 11 pm.

6. Lymphatic massage.

7. Check out tools used by some chiropractors, massage therapists and other complementary practitioners for detoxing:

- ion cleanse-a copper coil in a foot bath pulls toxins stored in muscles, joint and organs such as lymph and heavy metals through pores in the feet.

- bio-photon machine-glass tubes of inert gases activate cells in lymphatic system; this technique produces results deeper and more powerful than massage.

- various body scan machines that can detect viruses and bacteria and enhance the immune systems ability to cope.

- slow-cycling or "cool" laser. Used to heal wounds, reduce swelling from surgery and radiation burns and decrease scar tissue.

Emotional

We now know as a result of Candace Pert's work in neuro-immunology that emotions can remain stuck in the cells of our bodies for years. Emotions that are not released within an appropriate time after a triggering event can lead to both physical and mental illness. To detox the emotional field try:

- Dreamwork.
- Psychotherapy that has a physical or energetic component as opposed to traditional talk therapy.
- Journaling.
- Drawing or painting.
- Journeywork-a technique for traveling through layers of emotional debris in order to process and release the struck emotions that are contributing to disease. It is described by Brandon Bay in *The Journey* and *Freedom Is...*

Mental

- Read for information on how the body can heal itself.
- Take classes in energy medicine or energy psychology.
- Meditate 20 minutes 2x /day.
- Practice positive imagery.
- Count your blessings as often as possible throughout the day, everyday to develop an attitude of gratitude.

Spiritual

Detoxing the spiritual field also involves release. On this level, letting go equals surrender to God. The following are some of the things I did to facilitate that process:

- Classes in Contemplative Prayer.

- Weekly meetings with my Centering Prayer group.

- Daily prayer and meditation using both Christian methods as taught by Fr. Thomas Keating and Buddhist techniques as taught by Pema Chodrin.

- Daily prayers of gratitude and thanksgiving.

The goals of all these practices were the same:

- Surrender to God.

- Forgive self and others.

- Practice unconditional love toward self and others.

These, of course, are lifelong goals, but I believe that we need to make a conscious commitment to them in order to begin the process of healing.

BIBLIOGRAPHY

Alighieri, Dante. *The Divine Comedy,* trans. by John Ciardi. (W. W. Norton & Co., 1970).

Anderson, Greg. *Cancer: 50 Essential Things to Do.* (Plume/Penguin, 1999).

Baum, L Frank. *The Wizard of Oz.* (Jelly Bean Press, 1991)

Bays, Brandon. *Freedom Is Liberating Your Boundless Potential.* (New World Library, 2006)

Bays, Brandon. *The Journey.* (Fireside, 1999)

Benner, David G. *Surrender to LOVE.* (InterVarsity Press, 2003)

Bourgeault, Cynthia. *Centering Prayer and Inner Awakening.* (Cowley Publications, 2004).

Clift, Jean Dalby and Wallace B. *The Hero Journey in Dreams.* (Crossroad, NY, 1988).

Chodron, Pema. *Pema Chodron Audio Collection: Pure Meditation. Good Medicine, From Fear to Fearlessness.* (Sounds True, 2004).

Dale, Cyndi. *Advanced Chakra Healing.* (The Crossing Press, 2005)

Day, Lorraine, M.D. *"Cancer Doesn't Scare Me Anymore!"* (Video by ITV Direct, Inc.).

Fenske, Gina and Kate McGrath. *A Delicate Balance.* (Trianthus House Publishers, 2000).

Frost, Robert. *FROST.* (Everyman's Pocket Poets, Alfred Knopf, 1997).

Keating, Thomas. *Invitation to Love.* (Element, Inc., 1992).

Kidd, Sue Monk. *FIRSTLIGHT.* (Guideposts Books, 2006).

Kidd, *When the Heart Waits.* (Harper San Francisco, 1990)

Lamott, Anne. *Traveling Mercies*. (Anchor Books, 2000)

Menninger, William A. *The Process of Forgiveness*. (The Continuum International Publishing Group, 2004).

Murdock, Maureen. *The Heroine's Journey*. (Shambhala, 1990).

Myss, Caroline. *Energy Anatomy: The Science of Personal Power, Spirituality and Health*. (Sounds True*)*.

A New Treasury of Words to Live By. ed. by William Nichols. *(Simon and Schuster, 1959)*.

The Soul is Here for Its Own Joy. ed. by Robert Bly *(The ECCO Press, 1991)*.

Ten Poems to Change Your Life. ed. by Roger Housden. (Harmony Books, 2001).

A Treasury of the World's Best Loved Poems. (Avenal Books, 1961).

Rowling, J. K. *Harry Potter and the Deathly Hallows*. (Arthur A. Levine Books, 2007).

Rupp, Joyce. *Dear Heart Come Home*. (Crossroad Publishing Co., 1996)

Salzberg, Sharon. *The Force of Kindness: change your life with love and compassion*. (Sounds True, 2005).

Silberstein, Susan, PhD. *Hungry for Health*. (Infinity Publishing.com, 2005).

www.beatcancer.org. This website is recommended as a source of the most up-to-date information on ways to support the body's health and healing.

Made in the USA